The Gospel
with Extra Salt

Friends of Tony Campolo Celebrate

His Passions for Ministry

Edited by Joseph B. Modica

Judson Press

Valley Forge

The Gospel with Extra Salt
Friends of Tony Campolo Celebrate His Passions for Ministry

Unless otherwise indicated, Bible quotations in this volume are from the *New Revised Standard Version of the Bible,* copyright © 1989 by the Division of Christian Education of the National Council of the Churches of Christ in the United States of America. Used by permission. All rights reserved.

Bible quotations marked KJV are from *The Holy Bible, King James Version.*

Bible quotations marked NIV are from *HOLY BIBLE: New International Version,* copyright © 1973, 1978, 1984. Used by permission of Zondervan Bible Publishers.

Library of Congress Cataloging-in-Publication Data

The Gospel with extra salt : friends of Tony Campolo celebrate his passion for ministry / edited by Joseph B. Modica.
   p. cm.
   "Books by Tony Campolo": p.
   Includes bibliographic references.
   ISBN 0-8170-1313-X (pbk. : alk. paper)
   1. Church work. 2. Church and social problems. I. Campolo, Anthony. II. Modica, Joseph B.

BV4400.G67 2000
261.8-dc21   00-039083

Printed in the U.S.A.

06 05 04 03 02 01 00

10 9 8 7 6 5 4 3 2 1

To my wife, Marianne,
and our children,
Benjamin, Meredith,
Matthew, and Christopher,

And to the next generation of Tony Campolos:
The Simple Way Community,
Philadelphia

*[Jesus said,] "You are the salt of the earth,
but if the salt has lost its saltiness,
how can its saltiness be restored?
It is no longer good for anything,
but is thrown out and trampled underfoot."*
— Matthew 5:13

Contents

Foreword

IT WAS A DEFINING MOMENT. The message coming from my radio mixed a disarming humor with a scriptural call to keep the words of Jesus concerning the poor. I had often read Christ's teaching that only those who kept his words actually loved him, but Tony Campolo was applying the words of Jesus to real people in my time whom I was choosing to ignore. This sermon was a call to action for me—and for thousands of other generally well-meaning Christians who were too complacent about the poor. This was not just a call to action, it was an invitation to love Christ.

Many years have passed since I heard that sermon. Tony's books would further inspire me, as would many more of his sermons. All without fail would call me to Christ. In time I would come to know Tony personally, then intimately. It is a privilege to be his colleague and friend.

Tony has always been passionate about the poor—"eaten up with it," some might say. (Recall that the same thing was said of Jesus when he was driving the moneychangers out of the temple.) First-time visitors to Tony's office often find him fidgety. Finally, he will suggest that they take a ride. Within minutes Tony is engaged in meaningful conversations with people at Passyunk Homes, Cornerstone Christian Academy, and Urban Promise. Those are places where thousands of children know the love of Christ because of the various Evangelical Association for the Promotion of Education (EAPE) ministries initiated by Tony Campolo.

Lest we limit our description of Tony to inspiring preacher, talented author, and passionate caseworker, we should follow him to the classroom. His love of learning is broad and long. As a gifted student, he was invited to study with Einstein. As a young Ivy League professor, his classes filled up early. In four decades of teaching at Eastern College, he has always held students to the highest standards of performance in the integration of faith and reason. Faculty colleagues will attest to his voracious appetite for ideas in a continuing quest for knowledge.

The second chapter of Proverbs promises wisdom to those who both revere God and hunger for knowledge. Verse 9 explains that the result of such wisdom is an understanding of justice and equity. ("Then you will understand righteousness and justice and equity, every good path.") In those terms, Tony is a sage.

At the same time, Tony is a visionary and social entrepreneur. With the predictable volatility of those who have great minds and passionate hearts, he sees the future and creates problem-solving initiatives that transcend the stereotypes detractors would use to label him. For example, this "liberal" sociologist founded America's first faith-based economic development MBA program on the assumption that what the poor need most, besides spiritual renewal, is the dignity of gainful employment. In the midst of a protracted teachers' strike, this longtime advocate of public schools and teachers founded and funded a private Christian school for Philadelphia's neediest children. Frustrated by the growing self-centeredness of this generation of college students, this college professor challenged students around the world to "drop out" for one year and live, work, and worship in distressed urban neighborhoods.

In recent days, Tony has provided spiritual counsel to a U.S. president most evangelicals thought should resign from office in shame. However, the same Tony Campolo who has provided counsel has also gone to jail for protesting that president's policy on Aid to Families with Dependent Children.

The essays that follow in this book will help readers understand and enjoy the many dimensions of a complex and wonderful man. Scores of stories are not included, such as Tony's influencing a governmental decision to forgive certain debts to developing countries and persuading a major corporation to leave a Latin American community real means for progress before closing operations. Other stories, those written on the changed hearts of hundreds of thousands of people, will not be fully known until we celebrate them in heaven.

Importantly, there are stories to be written still. It is clear to a number of Tony's colleagues that he is growing more reflective and contemplative. Because of his high view of God's love and grace, he is often the recipient of questions asked by people of faith who are confused or in pain. The Lord promises peace to those who will bring him their burdens, and Tony is an agent of that peace. Therefore, I am looking forward to new and bold books and sermons for people of faith who are burdened and searching.

In the meantime, Tony, we all wish you and Peggy and Lisa and Bart and their families God's blessings and joy. May you continue to preach the gospel and share the love of Christ as only you can. May your vision and courage continue to inspire virtue in the rest of us. May you know how deeply you are loved and admired.

David R. Black
President
Eastern College

Acknowledgments

Many thanks to Randy Frame, acquisitions editor at Judson Press, for bringing this unique publishing project to fruition. I have appreciated Randy's counsel, encouragement, and perseverance during the literary birthing process.

Introduction

Joseph B. Modica

THIS BOOK OF ESSAYS honors a person who has reached a milestone—his sixty-fifth birthday. Moreover, he is in good health, continues to sprint from one speaking engagement to another, defies jetlag, writes many of his books at 30,000 feet in the air, and unabashedly preaches the same gospel of Jesus Christ that gripped and transformed him as a young man. He is also someone who resists caricature. A sociology professor? An author of more than twenty-five books? A prophet for the poor, exploited, and marginalized? An entrepreneur, who has begun more than a dozen national and international ministries? A dynamic preacher who fills churches to campgrounds? Someone who is an occasional guest on ABC's "Politically Incorrect"? Someone noted in Randall Balmer's recent book on American evangelicalism as a leading social activist? How does one define Dr. Tony Campolo?

The title of this book, *The Gospel with Extra Salt,* is perhaps one way of defining Tony Campolo: his unwavering emphasis on the difficult (and often avoided) sayings of Jesus, such as found in Matthew 25. We might echo the question, "Lord, when was it that we saw you hungry and gave you food, or thirsty and gave you something to drink? And when was it that we saw you a stranger and welcomed you, or naked and gave you clothing? And when was it that we saw you sick or in prison and visited you?" *(Matthew 25:37-39)*. But Tony's ministry has embodied Jesus' response: "Truly I tell you, just as you did it to one of the least of these who are members of my family, you did it to me" *(v. 40)*.

Furthermore, this book's subtitle offers yet another glimpse into the character of this man. Despite all the controversy surrounding him (some have suggested his middle initial stands for "controversial"!), Tony has many deep and committed friendships. Some of his friends have contributed to this volume, but many others could have also been included. Contributors were asked to write about an area of ministry that Tony has been passionate about, areas such as social justice, evangelism, and the church. David A. Fraser contributes to a biblical understanding of the family; Roberta Hestenes writes about the importance of gender issues in faith development; Gretchen Gaebelein Hull stresses the importance of inclusive language; Duffy Robbins assesses the present state of North American youth ministry; Ronald J. Sider offers a definition of the often elusive word "evangelical"; Bryan A. Stevenson addresses the injustice of capital punishment; and Jim Wallis presents strategies for overcoming national poverty. Finally, longtime mentor, pastor, and friend, John David Burton, has contributed a poetic afterword in honor of Tony.

In many ways, these essays exemplify the person and ministry of Tony Campolo. Seven years ago, when I first arrived as college chaplain at Eastern College, Tony's alma mater and home base, I was nervous about meeting the resident "celebrity"—the one who had written scores of books, preached around the world, and even coined the expression "It's Friday, But Sunday's Comin'." What I quickly discovered, however, is that the so-called celebrity is foremost a pastor—someone who calls his family, friends, and students from distant airports and countries to pray with them or sometimes just to say hello.

Tony, happy sixty-fifth birthday. We who are proud and honored to call ourselves your friends wish you Godspeed for continued health, vigor, and wisdom as you continue your preaching and teaching.

1/
Focus on the "Biblical Family": Sociological and Normative Considerations

David A. Fraser

WHAT ABOUT THE FAMILY?

What family is, isn't, ought to be, should or shouldn't include is the cause of much contemporary uproar. The definition of family has been stretched to encompass not only the nuclear family but extended families, gay marriages, single-parent households, blended families, and so on. The groups people live in and call family have changed in a veritable tidal wave. Over a thirty-year period in the United States there has been a tenfold increase in unmarried common-law couples, a dramatic rise in single-parent households, and a new openness in gay and lesbian partnering and parenting. There is no question that the family is changing.

So dramatic have the changes been that some see North America in the same sort of family decline that happened with the first-century Romans for some of the very same reasons. But is family change simply bad, or is it actually for the better? And is there a Christian perspective on some of these changes?

Almost no one celebrates the rise in divorce statistics, even while admitting that a certain percentage of those marriages needed such drastic surgery. Rising affluence has permitted women to get out of alcoholic and abusive, physically violent marriages. That is something to be celebrated.

Yet affluence has also funded easy marriage and easy divorce where there is no serious abuse. The changes in divorce laws since 1950 have opened a door that has liberated many from oppressive situations. At the same time, those new laws have been taken advantage of by people who marry for trivial reasons in the first place and end their marriages for many of the same trivialities. With such disruption experienced as children, young people are now putting marriage off, sensing it is a dangerous state to enter into. The average age of the first marriage has risen some six years in the last thirty years.

There is confusion about what counts as a family in the modern West. The pluralism of present definitions is matched with the power of rhetoric on all sides seeking to define "family" and debunk other notions. The legal and financial implications of the debate over what counts as family are profound for public life. But so too are the implications for the civil space that defines accepted and acceptable sexual and moral behavior. The moral space occupied by family has been so important to human life that we have no instances of communities without an array of formal and informal norms for structuring and organizing this area.

Yet in recent decades the conviction that all social rules are conventional, socially constructed, temporary arrangements of a given ideologically based group has undermined not only traditional norms but the notion of norms at all. It is rooted in a nearly absolute individualism. The new "rule" (if we may still speak of such) is that each person and each couple (or more) should have the right and responsibility to contract for their own way of embodying life's tasks and relationships. Everyone else should leave them alone. As the bumper sticker in Colorado Springs (Focus on the Family headquarters) puts it, "Focus on YOUR OWN family."

The less individualistic notion pushing new definitions of family is multiculturalism. It recognizes that humanity is a quilt of culturally differing groups (Laotians, Chinese, Australians, Iranians, Puerto

Ricans, African Americans, etc). Each should have the right to name its own patterns and live them out so long as they do not interfere with other groups' patterns and rights. The educational systems of North America are scrambling to produce textbooks and teachers who can relate to student bodies that may have representatives from dozens of differing cultural backgrounds.

This notion of multiculturalism and tolerance has taken the step further to include not only ethno-linguistic cultural groups but the alternative lifestyle enclaves within them such as gays and lesbians. On this approach, they too fall under the umbrella of the right to define their own civil space where they are to be left alone to form their own bonds and raise children in homosexually bonded "nuclear" families. The uproar since gay models of family life and child rearing were introduced into public school textbooks has been loud and rancorous.

Part of the new diversity of the family has even included tiny radical wings advocating a free-sex doctrine that includes parents initiating their own children into adult sexual practices at an early age. Far more common is the dismissal of the marriage certificate and public recognition of marriage commitments as meaningless. The percentage of those living together as couples without a formal wedding or civil documentation has grown tenfold in recent decades.

This essay reflects on some of the elements essential for a Christian perspective on the family. We want to know: Are there any norms that are permanent, transcultural, universal for the ideals and practice of Christians in all ages and all cultures? What do we make of the growing pressure within the church and outside it to validate and celebrate gay and lesbian marriages as equivalent to heterosexual marriages and families?

What's the Question?

It is often glibly said that "Christ is the answer." But what is the question?

When the average person asks, "But what about the family?" the issue being perused is usually a narrowly defined question: What about the traditional nuclear family made up of husband, wife, and their children (if they have any)? Even average Christians who ask what the Bible has to say about the family are usually thinking of the nuclear family. Normally modern Westerners take for granted that the nuclear family is definitive of what we mean when we say "family."

This reflects little awareness of the variety of family forms found in anthropological study of the spectrum of human social systems and cultures. Or at the least, if people have awareness, they consider much of that diversity as outside the essential core of what family is. So long as the nuclear element is intact and functioning properly, larger groupings, such as extended families, clans, sibs, moieties, lineages of various sorts, and so on are not germane to the real question at issue. That an anthropologist can even raise the valid question as to whether the nuclear family is empirically to be found in all societies is completely irrelevant to the actual issue that agitates people.[1]

When Christians make the claim that they are "biblical" in their orientation to this debate, they too seem to mean something far less than what the Bible takes to be "family." They have forgotten (or never known) the diversity of cultural patterns for the "family" exhibited in the Scripture. To be sure it is not a diversity as wide as all human culture. It is wide enough to provide both support for much of that diversity and a base for the critique of all human family forms to the present. It also proscribes some forms of arrangements people now wish to baptize with the name of "family."

This essay will reexamine the diversity of family patterns in the Bible with a view to giving an answer as to whether, what, and how limits on diversity in this social domain are set. Is there a "biblical" view of family? If so, what are its foundations and limits? Or is the diversity even in the Bible so great that we are left with virtually "anything goes" so long as love is present?

This is not a dead issue even within the conservative, evangelical ranks. In recent years Lewis Smedes, widely respected author of one of the most used texts in sexual ethics among evangelicals *(Sex for Christians)*, displays movement from a careful "no" to homosexual practice to a tentative "yes" to long-term committed monogamous homosexual bonding.[2] We want to ask whether we have biblical reasons for following this pilgrimage of Smedes to the same conclusions. Can such a thing as a Christian homosexual or lesbian marriage and family be normatively justified by Scripture?

David A. Fraser

Sociological Models of the Family

The first thing we need to note is that "family" is a very general category, because the way it is embodied in actual human societies is very complex and diverse. In size "family" ranges from two people to more than five hundred. "Family" deals in arrangements having to do with the relationships between generations, between those having sexual relations and procreating, between "blood" kin or consanguines and "in-laws" or affines, and between various other groupings of near "blood" relatives, such as clans, sibs, moieties, lineages, tribes, and so on. This is not to say there is an infinite variety or that all the actual diversity present even within a single society stands equally approved by its rules and laws. Nonetheless, the range of family systems is startling.[3]

There are a number of schemes that attempt to bring some general order to the unique features of the many family systems that social scientists have described. Emmanuel Todd provides one of the most recent and useful.[4] Todd seeks to show that family structures are related to political, philosophical, economic, and religious ideologies, not just to economic realities. He uses three criteria as the basis for his classification:

1. Liberty/authority: What is the basis of spouse choice—freedom of choice by the partners, oldest generation chooses, custom decides, or no rules?

2. Equality/inequality: Is the inheritance divided among the surviving children, or does only one child inherit; do the married children live with the parents?

3. Endogamy/exogamy: Is the social ideal to marry a close relative, or are there rules (e.g., prohibiting incest) that exclude this?

His seven types are: absolute nuclear, egalitarian nuclear, authoritarian, exogamous community, endogamous community, asymmetrical community, and anomic. To be sure, this scheme is a simplification of the empirical complexity (though all typologies are).[5] It is illustrative of the difficulty for social scientist or biblical scholar when asked to comment on "the family" situation. One wonders, "which family?"

When we start with an awareness of the various elements that are woven together to create a family system for any particular society,

Focus on the "Biblical Family"

Figure 1.1. Comparative Family Systems

Variables	Societies	
	First-Century Palestine	**Twentieth-Century United States**
Family Form	Endogamous community (multigenerational)	Absolute nuclear (dual-generational)
Spousal Choice	Controlled by custom and parents	Free choice by couple
Marriage Strategy	Endogamous (ideal)	Exogamous (by law)
Marriage Arrangement	Betrothal (families' negotiation)	Engagement (individuals' commitments)
Wedding Endowment	Formal: Dowry, indirect dowry, and bride-wealth	Informal: Family gifts
Postmarital Residence	Patrilocal (with groom's parents)	Neolocal (new household)
Cohabitation of Married Sons with Parents	Yes	No
Economic Function	Producing and consuming unit	Consuming unit
Geographical and Social Mobility	Severely restricted, thus closed networks	Limited restrictions, thus open networks
Inheritance Distribution	Oldest son: double Other sons: single Daughters: dowries	No inheritance rules as such; most property passed on by last wills and testaments

Based on K. C. Hanson and Douglas E. Oakman, *Palestine in the Time of Jesus: Social Structures and Social Conflicts (Minneapolis: Fortress Press, 1998), 22.*

we sense how difficult it is to leap directly from the pages of the Bible to the modern Western setting. The sorts of family systems (both in terms of ideals and practice) found in the New Testament world and now common in the modern world are miles apart so that it is not always obvious where to draw connections and conclusions. Figure 1.1 illustrates some of this distance by paralleling typical first-century Palestinian family patterns with twentieth-century North American patterns.

We need to be reminded of these differences when we read the comments of the New Testament writers. They deal with family roles, children, divorce, the relative weight of loyalty to family when it conflicts with discipleship, the tensions within families, questions of multiple marriages, and so on. In so doing, they refer first of all to the endogamous community family of the first century. They are dealing also with the pressures and threats to that family system that came within the first-century world.

If we transfer the insight of New Testament writers on Palestinian and Roman family systems to the modern absolute nuclear form, some conceptual and theological bridges will certainly have to be built. We must first be fair and insightful on how the teachings of Jesus and the apostles dealt with their family systems. We must understand the attitudes, standards, and vices that accompanied those systems before pronouncing on a biblical view that may help us cope with similar matters that are part of the Western absolute nuclear form of the family.

A step further in any pilgrimage for a "focus" on the biblical family is understanding, not only the first-century Palestinian family, but the family structures that were present in the larger Roman world. One of the tensions between Jewish Christians and Gentile Christians in apostolic times had to do, not only with whose food rules governed Christian fellowship, but whose kinship sensibilities were to be observed in marriage arrangements.

As it turns out, the Jewish rules of marriage that forbade certain close relatives as marriage partners differed from the typical Roman kinship rules. When the apostolic church asked the question, "What about the family?" one issue that bubbled up within the house churches had to do with suitable marriage partners. As parents arranged the marriages for their children to other believers, whom could they select? Which partners might be considered "incestuous" or too close a relative for marriage purposes?

This is reflected in the apostolic letter sent by James and the leaders of the Jerusalem church to the Gentile believers *(Acts 15:20-21, 29)*. In this case, Moses is cited as the basis for placing limits on Gentile Christian practices that might scandalize their Jewish Christian brothers and sisters. Included in the restrictions were abstinence from the contaminations of idols (a reference to food offered at the shrines of idols), "whatever has been strangled and from blood" (i.e., animals that have been strangled with the blood remaining in the flesh), and sexual immorality (often translated inaccurately as "fornication").

What is often not noticed is that these are the Mosaic restrictions of Leviticus 17:8-18:30 put on the alien (i.e., the Gentile) who resided among Israel.[6] The restrictions in Leviticus 18 deal with sexual immorality, specifically forbidden degrees of kinship relations that are considered incestuous by Israel, and other disallowed sexual practices (specifically male homosexuality and sexual relations with animals). All are considered defiling, depraved, abominable, and perverted.[7] All are referenced in the Jerusalem decree and made normative by this early council for fostering Jewish-Gentile Christian fellowship.

Furthermore, these rules ban incest, idolatry, bestiality, and homosexuality specifically as dishonoring to God, not simply as disruptive of family stability of a certain family form. These proscriptions are rooted in a sensibility deeper than the patriarchy of an extended family system. They have to do with the nature and character of the God who created human beings and who calls them into a covenant that disciplines their sexuality and family arrangements. The Creator's right to name the nature of creation, even after it is fallen and distorted by sin, remains the dominant motive in this legislation.

Family Diversity in the Bible

A quick overview of some of the major elements of family patterns in the Bible will reveal that the Bible does not prescribe a single, simple pattern for all family systems everywhere. Rather, it regulates all family systems according to a normative set of ideals that can be spelled out with some precision and confidence.

In terms of vocabulary, Old Testament Hebrew has no word that corresponds precisely to "family" in the sense that is used in English. One might think of Old Testament terms translated at one place or another as "family" as a sort of inverted cone. At the bottom is the smallest unit, the *bêth āḇ,* the father's house.[8] This was the small settlement unit that is composed of a "father," his wife (wives of various sorts), his unmarried sons and daughters, his married sons and their wives and children, along with any slaves and servants. It was the extended family or household that functioned to produce and consume most of the primary goods necessary for continued health and participation in the ritual functions of Israel. It was a multigenerational, patrilineal, patrilocal residential unit whose members supported each other and arranged for most family matters, from education to the provision of dowry and bride-wealth for its members.

Just above the *bêth āḇ* is the *mišpāḥâ,* the clan. This was a sort of protective association made up of a number of *bayitim* (patrilineal extended households). Normally they lived in the same general area. They functioned to provide mutual assistance to extended households belonging to the clan and to supply young warriors when assembling for war. They also constituted the local judicial bodies that dealt with crime and conflict within the clan. Preferential endogamous marriage rules meant that many if not most marriages were within the clan as its households cemented bonds with each other by exchanging sons and daughters (or at least within clans belonging to the same tribe).

The next-to-largest unit was the *šēḇeṭ* or *maṭṭeh,* the tribe. This was a relatively autonomous association of segmented extended families, usually made up of fifty or more "clans." They were interlocked through intermarriage, mutual aid, common worship, and levies of warriors supplied to the army of Israel. The twelve tribes together made up the highest level political and cultural unit known as Israel and were drawn together by Aaronite and Levite lineages that bound the whole into a common worship of Yahweh as their covenant God.

At times the term house *(bayiṯ)* is used for the house of Israel (referring to the whole population), the house of Judah (referring to the

"tribe"), and even the house of Jesse (referring to the extended household of Jesse and his wives, children, married sons, and their children).
In all cases, the integrating notion is that people are related in terms of
the solidarity of kinship, near and far, that sets them apart from other
ethnic units. The common ancestors are first of all Abraham and Sarah
through Isaac and Jacob and then, for each tribal grouping, one of the
sons of Jacob (or grandsons in the case of Joseph).

In all of these family structures, there is no freestanding nuclear unit.
But this is only the beginning of the picture we find as we move
through the Bible.[9]

Patriarchal Era

The patriarchal era provides us with the smallest amount of information as to family patterns and rules. Some practices noted later are disallowed by Mosaic legislation. Nonetheless, we find the fundamental
pattern of an endogamous, patrilineal, patrilocal extended family pattern that practices polygyny. Much of this form of family system continues through Israel's history, even while some close kin are removed
from the preferential pool of candidates and proscribed later.

Endogamy was evidently very important as this original set of
households moved from their homeland into Palestine and then
Egypt.[10] Marriage within the patrilineage was practiced as the preferential rule, though when a parallel cousin was not found, other women
could be eligible partners. Levirate marriage (marriage to the childless
widow of a brother to raise up descendants for his name and preserve
property in the lineage) was already in practice (Genesis 38:6-26; see
Deuteronomy 25:5-10). In addition, a man could have not only several primary wives, but legal secondary wives (often these were slaves or
captives from warfare) and concubines. In the case of the patriarchs,
some were the property (part of the dowry) of their wives (Genesis 16;
29:24, 29; 30:3-13). This appears to be a form of concubinage. In this
case concubines/handmaids were used to produce children that would
have been counted as belonging to their mistresses (a sort of early sur-
rogate motherhood).

One pattern also present is the use of the marriage bond as a strategy for family benefit in the face of the more powerful settled popu-
lations. For example, the patriarchs seem willing to offer their wives

and married daughters to powerful urbanites in order to further their own political and economic well-being. Abraham does this with Sarah *(Genesis 12:10-20; 20:2-18)*, Lot with his daughters *(Genesis 19:12-16, 31-38)*, and Jacob with his daughter Dinah *(Genesis 34; note Jacob's later curse on Simeon and Levi for their aggressive vengeance in Genesis 49:5-7)*.

Prostitution was present in this time (cf. Judah's entrapment by his daughter-in-law Tamar in *Genesis 38)*, but its extent and nature cannot be assessed from the little said of it in Genesis. This incident suggests sacred prostitution, which we find clearly with the cult of Astarte later. But we know little of its nature in patriarchal time. Furthermore, the narrative concerning Judah and Tamar focuses on Judah's unrighteousness in not arranging a levirate marriage for Tamar rather than his visiting what is described as a "temple prostitute" *(Genesis 38:22)*.

Israel and Monarchical Israel

Israel and monarchical Israel exhibit an extension and intensification of many of these patterns. It is in this time that the full range of family structures, from the father's house *(bêth āb)* to the twelve "tribes" of Israel, develop into their full forms.

In brief, Israel is a multilayered (father's extended household, the clan, the tribe, and all Israel) family system that is ordered by patrilineages headed by the senior living males of multigenerational households. Patrilocality marked marriage residence. Marriages were arranged by the household elders using rules that seem to lead in the direction of an expanded set of preferential partners (i.e., disapproving of the close kin marriages common in the patriarchal era), with preferential in-marriage within tribes and between or within clans. While there is evidence even here of intermarriage outside Israel (to Edomites, Canaanites, Philistines, etc.), these were normally disapproved family alliances.

Levirate marriage continues, as well as the institution of the "kinsmen redeemer" for cases such as Naomi and Ruth, in which brothers of the widow's husband are not available. In any case, prescribed levirate marriage is one indication that polygyny could at times be involuntary. It served as a sort of "social security" net for women who were widowed young as well as an economic institution keeping property in the patrilineage. Polygyny is found in royal forms in the households of the kings and nobility.

We read that in Gideon's time many wives were an expression of wealth and success *(Judges 8:30)*. David had six named wives, as well as a number of unnamed wives and concubines. Solomon developed a full-scale royal harem of seven hundred wives and three hundred concubines. Much of Solomon's excess was tied to using marriage as a means of sealing political alliances. Yet there is discomfort with this extreme expansion of the custom of many wives *(Deuteronomy 17:17)*. Mosaic legislation recognizes the difficulties of equality of treatment *(Deuteronomy 21:15-17)* as well as the bad moral influence it might have. A husband's favoritism might easily pit wife against wife.

The women in this era appear to be so embedded in the honor of the males of the patrilineage that there is no indication of the earlier use of wives or married daughters to manipulate the more powerful and wealthy for the household's interests. On the contrary, the marriage strategy appears rather to be to gain wives and daughters but not give them away *(Exodus 34:14-16; Deuteronomy 7:1-6; Joshua 23:11-13)*. The sort of "sexual hospitality" that appears present in the patriarchal era is now outlawed *(Exodus 20:14,17; Deuteronomy 5:18,21; 2 Samuel 3:6-11)*. Sacred prostitution by either males or females is forbidden *(Deuteronomy 23:17-18)*. Concubines are identified with their male holders so that going into them usurps their power and may create an outrage similar to incest *(2 Samuel 16:20-22; 1 Kings 2:13-17)*.

Elder males (fathers) continue to be the decisive figure in marriage and family affairs. For example, eloping with an unmarried and unbetrothed girl does not make a marriage *(Exodus 22:16-17; cf. Deuteronomy 22:23-29 for variations)*. The father of the girl still has the right to decide whether to legitimate the event. Marriage arrangements are placed in the hands of the patrilineage, not in the will of the couple who may wish to marry.

Legislation in Leviticus makes a number of practices or actions abominations: adultery *(Leviticus 18:20; 20:10)*; "sexual hospitality" *(Leviticus 19:29)*; Israelite women as slave-wives *(Leviticus 25:44-46)*; male homosexuality *(Leviticus 18:22; 20:13)*; priestly marriages with a woman who has been used for "sexual hospitality" or divorced *(Leviticus 21:7, 13-14; cf. Ezekiel 44:22);* and sexual relations with close kin, literally, "inner flesh of his flesh" *(Leviticus 18:6-18: 20:11-21).*

Postexilic Israel

Postexilic Israel shows a sensitivity to the Torah regulations that had been violated, leading to the disastrous history of the exile of both the northern kingdom of Israel and the southern kingdom of Judah. When the exiles returned under Ezra and Nehemiah, there was a strong insistence on breaking marriages with "foreign" women and returning to endogamous patterns that disallowed marriage outside of legitimated "Jewish" households *(Ezra 9-10; Nehemiah 9-10).* Nonetheless, the basic patterns set in preexilic Israel and canonized in Mosaic Torah appear to govern the basic practices of this era. There is little evidence as to the degree to which diaspora involvements led to the adopting of Gentile customs in marriage and family roles.

The book of Sirach (about 150 B.C.) in general confirms the older patrilineal pattern. Fathers (or mothers in the absence of fathers) arranged marriages. Some texts advise early marriage for sons *(Ecclesiasticus 7:23)* and avoidance of unmarried women *(9:5),* married women *(9:8-9),* and prostitutes *(9:6).* Daughters are vulnerable and a potential threat to the honor of the male head of the household and thus are to be married off shortly after the onset of menses *(26:10-12; 42:9-11).*

The purpose of marriage retains the Old Testament accent on children, namely, the production of a holy seed (Ecclesiaticus, Tobit, Judith; cf. Tobit 8:7 for the motivation for sexual union). To enter into marriage for reasons of the beauty of the person or wealth of the bride's family was considered by the rabbis as immorality. Jesus insults his contemporaries by calling them an "adulterous generation" *(Matthew 12:39; 16:4; Mark 8:38),* a reference, not only to the ease of divorce, but to the sort of marriage-go-round we see in the elite families such as the Herodians.[11] Polygamy was a continuing practice in this era, again largely among the wealthy and powerful.

Apostolic Christian Patterns

Apostolic Christian patterns are mixed simply because the Christian movement includes members from both Jewish and Gentile backgrounds.

Nonetheless, we see a patrilineal pattern household present in both Palestine and in much of the Roman world.

Most frequently mentioned in the New Testament is the "household," that central, multigenerational group that included not only the master *(kurios, despotēs)* or paterfamilias, but his wife, children, slaves, and other dependents (employees, servants, even clients). Marriages were arranged by the male leaders of these extended groups who sometimes continued to interfere in the marriages of their daughters. The authority given to the male head was strikingly strong in that the paterfamilias in the Roman household had rights to sell his son, to expose unwanted babies, and even to kill some members of his household with impunity.

When we read the "household codes" *(Ephesians 5:21-6:9; Colossians 3:12-4:1; 1 Peter 2:17-3:8)*, we get a sense of a church movement struggling with making sense of a family system that had harshness and difficulty in it for its weaker members. The role relationships of paterfamilias and wife, of parents and children, of master/mistress and slave are addressed in terms of the difference it makes when one is "in Christ." In every case, the more powerful family member in the role set has that power limited and his behavior grounded in the servant attitude of Christ himself.

It is not insignificant that the church movement was largely built around "house churches" and that the apostolic Christians thought of themselves as an extended family (the "household" of God). The centrality of the family in Israel is translated into the ideals of the sort of social community that was to grow up into Christ himself.[12]

There is little explicit commentary in the New Testament on the issues of polygyny (though Pauline legislation holds up the monogamous elder/bishop as ideal for leadership). More is focused on a theology of sexuality *(1 Corinthians 5-7)* and on the changes that come with the arrival of the messianic agent. While the Old Testament has no word for "bachelor" and stresses the importance of childbearing, the New recognizes the validity of singleness *(Matthew 19:12; 1 Corinthians 7)*. Because the Savior has arrived, bearing children takes on a new meaning within marriage.

With the transcending of ethnicity and purity rules, we also see a shift in the rules of endogamy. The stress now turns to marrying those who are believers, members of the fictive kinship unit known as the household of God. The new clan is religious, not ethnic. Marriage changes in its function from having to do with family alliances and the promotion of one's own interests through advantageous marriages to establishing households that image the coming community of the kingdom of God.

This has been only a brief, rapid tour. But it has turned up polygyny, arranged marriages, concubinage, levirate marriage, and slave marriage, as well as legislation banning violations of the variety of marriage bonds created by these extended-family, patrilineal patterns. The biblical family encompasses far more than the nuclear family of modern concern.

Evaluating the Biblical Families and Patterns

Once we are fully aware of the range of possible sorts of marriage and family arrangements, we can ask more adequately what the biblical viewpoint is on all this diversity. Are all these arrangements equal in the eyes of God, or are some sorts of family arrangements privileged within a larger scheme of God's will? We know Jesus scored the misuse of the Mosaic permission for divorce (some made it a prescription commanding divorce in given situations and expanded the grounds for a legitimate divorce to trivialities; *see Matthew 19:3-12).*[13] He explained its significance as a less-than-ideal accommodation made by God because of the hardness of people's hearts. But it was still a permission given by God for difficult marriages. Its abuse did not abolish the fact that God sanctions some divorce.

Jesus clearly worked with a notion that even within biblical material all things are not on the same normative level. There is an original and continuing intention of God for sexuality, marriage, and family. It is that ideal I want to identify and relate to some of the sociological diversity I have briefly described.

I will be working with what Charles Kraft calls the tether model.[14] This model is a metaphor based on tethering animals with a rope and stake so that they are able to graze only in a given circle within the limits allowed by the rope. Or it can be thought of in terms of the game of tetherball. In this case there is a pole to which a rope is attached with a ball on the end. The goal of the game is to wrap the rope around the pole while your opponent seeks to do the same in the opposite direction. Here too there is a circumference set by the length of the rope attached to the pole.

The notion is that there is a range of acceptable diversity and variation around a biblical ideal that may be less than ideal but is not sinful (see Figure 1.2). Like the tether stake or pole, the center point is the ideal. Yet around it is a set radius that marks a border or circumference. What lies beyond that circumference is out of bounds. In this metaphor, what lies outside the border is sinful and not acceptable.

It is impossible to make sense of either the normative or descriptive diversity in scriptural material with a simple dichotomy of ideal versus sinful. On the tether model there are three arenas: the biblical ideal, the less than ideal but not sinful, and the sinful. The ideal serves as the ultimate good in a given domain, a good that was intended in creation and will be realized in the coming kingdom of God.[15] But there is an acceptable range of departure from that ideal in the fallen world that God allows and regulates in light of the ideal itself.

In considering the biblical family, we have discovered that the range of acceptable patterns is astonishing when considered against the naive notion that the absolute nuclear family is "God's pattern." How do we make sense of what was permitted not only in actual empirical practice, but in the Mosaic legislation?

Without developing the whole argument in this chapter, we can identify the core ideal as it is found in Genesis 2:24. Christ appeals in order to relativize Mosaic divorce legislation: "Therefore a man leaves his father and his mother and clings to his wife, and they become one flesh." It is the passage Paul develops in Ephesians 4:25-33 as the prescriptive pattern for understanding, not only human marriage, but the nature of the relationship between Christ and the church.[16]

Whatever marriage pattern and family system exists in a given cultural group, it is intended to serve as an imager of the sort of union that exists between Christ and the church. In Old Testament terms it is a "one-flesh" ideal that is celebrated in vivid tones in the Song of Solomon. As Trobisch so eloquently develops it, the biblical ideal has three facets that frequently are only realized one-sidedly in cultural

Figure 1.2. The Tether Model

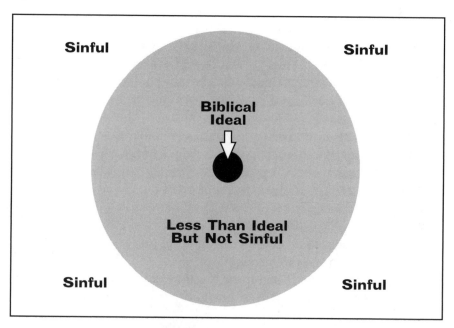

Based on Charles H. Kraft, Christianity in Culture: A Study in Dynamic Biblical Theologizing in Cross-Cultural Perspective *(Maryknoll, N.Y.: Orbis, 1981), 398.*

ideals and actual practice. These are what he calls wedlock ("leaving"), sexual union ("one flesh"), and love ("cleave"): "Marriage is like this skillful performance [of three jugglers giving and receiving balls from each other in a triangle]. Its life depends upon the interplay between the legal, the personal and the physical aspects of the relationship."[17]

The legal is wedlock, the formal, public recognition and approval of the community. This is stressed and made central by many traditional family systems that define marriage as a linkage of family interests. The physical is the sexual, the one-flesh union. It has been so exalted by modern notions that marriage licenses and public approval are frequently seen as irrelevant or only a formality. The relationship is continued so long as the sexual is exciting and fulfilling. When it no longer is a torrid flame, the partners seek others. The personal is the cleaving love that energizes both marriage and sex. It pushes the relationship toward physical expression and needs the security of a publicly validated, legally binding wedding.

Yet there is a great deal of confusion and difficulty over these three: sex, love, and marriage. Traditional arranged marriages enter the relationship through the public, family-guided door, with hope that love will develop and with the expectation that children will issue. Yet stressing wedlock unduly distorts the original intent. Marriage comes to be used for political alliances, social climbing, and the production of heirs to a lineage. Marriages are seen as incomplete without children. Barrenness is grounds for divorce or for concubinage. Yet in this passage the couple is complete without children. There is a period at the end of Genesis 2:24 with no mention of children. Nor does this give support to the Roman Catholic view of sexual relations as being meaningful and full only when and if engaged in with the intentionality of having children. Yet wedlock can exist without love. When there is only wedlock and sex, the marriage is empty. Legality by itself does not a marriage make. It needs the other two elements.

Modern notions stress sexual compatibility as the gate through which marriage ought to be entered. Contraceptives have made sexual relations easy and almost "safe." Hollywood portrays the "chemistry" of sexual attraction as the basis for both love and the justification for marriage. Yet common law "marriages" frequently are fraught with the insecurity that comes due to the refraining from the irrevocable and permanent step of wedlock. Rather than strengthening the tie, sex and love in the absence of wedlock actually increase the rate of breakups between couples, even after they finally take the plunge and marry. A common law marriage becomes a sort of "stolen" marriage without firm legal foundations. Legally protected and publicly bonded, a couple can have their ups and downs in the passion of both love and sex and know that they have made mutual promises and vows. Without the legalities and the public vows, a door is always open through which one or the other partner may disappear when times are difficult.

The biblical ideal stresses the love gate as the way into and through marriage in a fallen world. While God's will is a dynamic interplay of all three of these elements, it is love that finally motivates the fulfillment of the long-term vows and commitments made in wedlock and covers a multitude of sins and boredoms that come to every couple in their sex life.

Yet this triad of elements is flexible and creative enough that it can suit a variety of cultures and individual situations. The public-family element of wedlock, the personal-emotional element of love, and the physical-sexual element of one flesh can be played out in a variety of ways in different cultures.

Genesis 2:24 is a theology of sexuality rooted in creation's intent and ideal that provides the final norm for all family systems and arrangements. It allows us also to begin to appreciate both the patience and tolerance of God in working with us in our fallen family systems. At the same time we can make more sense of the trajectory and change in the Bible as it legislates and celebrates humans and their struggles in marriage.

The biblical ideal is a union that is between a man and a woman involving "leaving" the family of origin (the marital tie is to be stronger than the kinship tie), "cleaving" to each other (an exclusive, lifelong commitment undergirded by self-giving love), and "becoming one flesh" (an ongoing and growing intimacy that is expressed sexually).

If this is the ideal, then we can move quickly to place a number of the patterns observed in the other two categories of the "tether model." While polygamy is a legitimated and publicly recognized form of marriage, it is not held up in any of the biblical literature as an ideal. Rather, it is an acceptable family pattern that is less than ideal. Its dangers are spelled out in Scripture, and legislation limits its abuses and misuses. It violates the exclusivity of the marriage bond by creating multiple bonds for one of the partners. In the modern world polygamy is dying out because it is uneconomical and loses its functions in the urban context. Monogamy, when lived out well, is closer to God's ideal than polygamy.

The same can be said for marriage forms that place partners in the union in different statuses (such as primary legal and secondary legal spouses; or legitimate but not legally binding relationships such as concubines in some situations). Levirate marriage is similar. These are less than ideal, though acceptable patterns in social worlds where they function to provide home and security for a sector of women who otherwise would be exposed to far more draconian conditions (female captives in warfare; the young widow without recourse for support). There is wedlock in these cases, but it is of a sort that has inadequate protections for the secondary wives and weakens the primary and original tie. Such arrangements can only partially meet the ideals of exclusivity, justice, and security essential to long-term committed marriage. When tension arises between wives, the secondary partners invariably are the losers (as in the case between Sarah and Hagar—*Genesis 21:8-21*). Marriages of a single legal and social status are closer to God's ideal than the sort of double- and triple-tiered arrangements allowed in many Old Testament instances.

The language used for a number of practices makes them such clear violations of the marriage and family ideals that they cannot be placed in the less than ideal but acceptable category: adultery, rape, sexual relations with animals, prostitution (both "sexual hospitality" and sacred prostitution), and divorce for trivial reasons.

More needs to be said on each of these categories and the reasons for placing them in one of the three categories. In any given case, the actual embodiment of what is categorically acceptable may render it in practice sinful and unacceptable. Divorce is at times better than the sustaining of a rancorous and abusive marriage (as Paul recognized in *1 Corinthians 7*). There are polygamous families that embody more grace, love, and justice than some monogamous marriages. The care shown for widows and the poor in the institution of levirate marriage often outshines the impersonal and flawed system of social services available in modern societies with nuclear family ethics. So the placement of these family patterns is meant only to be illustrative and categorical, not universal or unexceptional.

The Controverted Question of Homosexual "Marriage and Family"

On this model, homosexual "marriage and family" (long term bonded, socially recognized, ecclesially approved, civilly sanctioned monogamous ties) is to be placed outside the less-than-ideal-but-not-sin category. From a biblical viewpoint, homosexual relationships are clearly and consistently considered a form of sexual immorality. The biblical view is through and through heterosexual in its vision of marriage and family.

This has been the pattern evident from the earliest vision of creation through all stages of the people of God, from the patriarchs to the contemporary church (and the traditional position of all the major bodies, whether Roman Catholic, Protestant, Anglican, Orthodox, or Non-Western Indigenous). The servants of the covenant of the God of the Bible have never had any other custom than heterosexual marriage and family, even when they existed in intimate contact with cultures that allowed homosexual practice and marriage. Those now within the church who seek to overturn this do so at great peril. The zeal to correct harsh and inappropriate attitudes toward gays and lesbians is a good agenda for justice. At the same time, pushing for a change in sexual ethics and ecclesial practice can only produce a serious compromise of the authority of Scripture and a diminishing of its overall vision for sexuality and family.

The reasons leading to this conclusion are as follows.

1. The strictures of the Old Testament on homosexual practice are a matter of a larger vision of the meaning of sexuality, not simply the specifics of fertility, religious practices, or cultural peculiarities. The Old Testament does mention bisexual activity of males in general *(Genesis 19:1-11; Judges 19:22-26)* and male cult prostitutes *(1 Kings 14:22-24; 15:12; 22:46; 2 Kings 23:7)*. It forbids both sorts of activity *(Leviticus 18:22; 20:13; Deuteronomy 23:17)*.

In dealing with male homosexual activity, Leviticus places it within the general discourse of incest, the giving of children to Molech (idolatry of a particularly objectionable sort), bestiality, as well as other forms of sexual immorality. The banning of it along with incest and bestiality is tied explicitly to the honoring of Yahweh as a covenant people and being distinctive in lifestyle from the surrounding Egyptians and Canaanites *(Leviticus 18:2-5)*. Female homosexual activity is not directly commented on in the Old Testament.

2. Postexilic and first-century Judaism consistently rejected homosexual activity and marriage found in their diaspora environments.

Charles Talbert summarizes some of the evidence in this way:[18]

> Ancient Judaism was likewise uniformly negative toward homosexuality. Wis. of Sol. 14:26 speaks about idolatry producing evil results, such as disorder in marriage, adultery, and confusion of sex. Philo condemns pederasty in particular *(On the Special Laws 3.37-39; Questions and Answers on Genesis 4.37-38)* and homosexuality in general as a perversion akin to adultery *(On Abraham 26.134-36)*. "Do not be a sodomite or an extortioner or a murderer," exhorts the Sibylline Oracles *(2.73)*. It later states that Jews do not hold unholy intercourse with boys as do Phoenicians, Egyptians, Latins, Greeks, and others *(3.591-99)*, and it links idolatry with homosexual acts, prostitution, and incest *(5.386-433)*. In his vision of the place of torment, Enoch is told it is for those "who dishonor God, who on earth practice sin against nature, which is child-corruption after the sodomitic fashion" *(2 Enoch 10.4)*. Josephus refers to the unnatural vice rampant among the people of Elis and Thebes, incest and homosexuality, which were justified by the examples of the Greek gods *(Against Apion 2.273-75)*. Pseudo-Phocylides says, "Do not give yourself over, against nature, to unpermitted love. Man's love to man is even detested by animals" *(109-10)* and "Do not have illicit intercourse or stir up a passion for another male, or lay plots, or stain your hand with blood" *(3-5)*. Although the homosexuality condemned by ancient Judaism included pederasty, it was by no means limited to the corruption of boys. Sifra on Lev. 18:3, for example, condemns homosexual marriages, both male and female, among the Egyptians and Canaanites.

3. Greco-Roman practice was explicit and complex, and it included much more than pederasty.[19]

Greek literature and archaeology provide pervasive evidence for the public place of human sexuality. Monumental phalluses were used as boundary markers. Small posts or pillars (ithyphalluses) with the heads of Hermes and equipped with erect penises were "as common in the streets as fire hydrants are today. Representations of male and female genitalia were used to promote fertility...and also to scare away baneful influences."[20] Homosexuality was present and practiced by both males and females. As Jeffrey Henderson notes:

> The Greeks considered it perfectly natural and normal that a man or youth would feel, and seek to gratify, sexual desire for the other (usually younger) males. There is also strong evidence to suggest that a similar homosexual object choice was open to females....Not only was homosexual sentiment pervasive in Greek culture, but homosexuality, at least in the late archaic and early classical periods, also played an important role in the transition of boys (and probably girls, too) from childhood into adulthood. It was in no way felt to interfere with heterosexual enjoyment or with a happy marriage.[21]

Almost all of Greek sexuality is structured by status considerations, so that adult male citizens were placed on a different level than women, slaves, and children. The love of a man and woman are inferior in Plato's *Symposium* to homosexual love between males. Only such male love could fulfill the nature of a male (cf. also *Phaedrus)*. Yet homosexual relations were not supposed to interfere with or substitute for heterosexuality in marriage, and those who could not stop the pursuit of younger males or who themselves acted as passive partners were considered "womanish" and "slavish."

Sappho's poetry is homosexual in nature and may indicate some of the sorts of "training" young girls were given by older women in preparation for marriage. The name of the island of her birth, Lesbos, has provided the popular designation for female homosexuality, lesbianism. But the conviction in this case was that it was a behavior to be given up upon marriage.

Roman attitudes were divided. On the one hand was the more ancient and puritanical notion that sexual passions should be restrained and contained. As Talbert summarizes, "Traditional Roman values opposed homosexuality among citizens *(Livy, 38-39; Suetonius 'Caligula'; Juvenal Satires 6)*. Homosexual activity had been illegal since the *Lex Scantinia* (either 223 or 149 B.C.), but the law was usually invoked only for political purposes."[22]

On the other side is an extremely permissive celebration of virtually any and all sorts of sexual activity. Petronius's *Satyricon* chronicles four bisexually promiscuous main characters and an array of lust-ridden minor players.[23] Pompeii is full of ribald graffiti, phallic and ithyphallic images. Its painting, reliefs, statues, and metalwork display a riot of explicitly erotic scenes.

Over time the Romans were Hellenized and came to copy the Greek idealization of homosexuality (Plutarch *Eroticus;* Plautus *Pseudolus* and *The Braggert Warrior;* Suetonius, "Nero," on Nero's homosexual marriage; Juvenal *Satires* 2, a reference to a homosexual marriage; cf. Hadrian's liaison with Antoninus). At times homosexuality was taken (cynically) to be an alternative to marriage to a woman (Juvenal *Satires* 6) or just as a convenient liaison (Petronius *Satyricon*).

There was a double standard in that the Romans viewed female homosexual activity as much worse than male homosexuality. Such behavior among women was labeled masculine and unnatural (Ovid, *Metamorphoses* 9.666ff.; Seneca the Elder, *Controversiae* 1.2.23; Martial, *Epigrams* 1.90; 7.67, 70). In contrast, male homosexuality was not frowned on so long as it met some conditions: one must take the active, physically penetrating role. The adolescent must be the passive partner (who could not be a freeborn Roman citizen). It was to be discreet, voluntary, and not threaten public funds.

There was, to be sure, a trade in beautiful boys for both prostitution and concubinage.[24] As Krenkel summarizes,

> young men would keep boys as concubines, putting them aside when they married or continuing the liaison even after they had wed (as Hadrian continued his relationship with Antinous). Intercourse between masters and their male slaves was normal and in accord with the male-dominated society (Seneca the Elder, *Controversiae* 4, preface 10: "Sexual servicing is a crime for the freeborn, a necessity for a slave, and a duty for the freedman." Slave boys were sent out to attract customers especially in harbor towns on the docks....Beautiful boys were captured and imported by carriage and ship, sold and hired out (Juvenal, 9.132; Aristophanes *Equites* 1069; Catullus, 106; Martial, 9.59;

Plautus, *The Weevil* 382-384). Roman youngsters encountered homosexuality at school [long before they encountered a public life where it might be used to recruit a patron] (Quintilian, *Education of an Orator* 1.2.4; 2.2.1-5, advised parents not to send their boys to schools because of the pederasty that flourished).

In summary, the Greco-Roman world in which Jews were a diaspora and into which the Christian movement spread, was a comparatively highly eroticized and publicly explicit culture in its sexuality. The evidence of homosexuality among both men and women as well as pederasty is clear enough. There were cases of homosexual "marriage," though rare compared with homosexual concubinage and ongoing liaisons. The negative comments in the culture and in the New Testament are directed not simply against pederasty but also against adult male and female homosexuality.

4. Apostolic and early Christianity followed the pattern of the Old Testament and ancient Judaism by placing homosexual activity (and meaning more than pederasty) of both genders in the category of the fruit of alienation from God and the expression of sin. While there may be question as to whether the homosexual hesitations and condemnations of the Old Testament are because of its association with idolatry, there is little question that Paul's considerations are broad and deep.[25]

There are only four direct references to homosexuality in the New Testament. Romans 1:26-27 speaks of both male and female homosexuality and ties it to the rejection of the Creator and falling into idolatry. The Greco-Roman gods/goddesses and heroes were all represented as erotic, lustful agents who did much the same as their human counterparts but, because of their power, got away with it. Some types of forbidden sexual activity are attributed to them as well: adultery, rape, fornication, bestiality, sodomy, and even mutilation and incest. Paul's connection of sexual misbehavior and idolatry is rooted in part in the encouragement and modeling of such behavior by the gods and goddesses of his day.

Paul's theological rationale is broader than Leviticus (or makes part of the rationale of Leviticus more explicit). Such behavior is more than the expression of idolatrous worship. It is part and parcel of the exchanging of the Creator and his intentions for the creation *(Romans 1:25ff.)*. Thus, every homosexual act is "unnatural" *(1:26)*. This is not because it cuts across the sexual orientation of the homosexual or Old Testament law, but because it violates the Creator's scheme for male and female sexuality in creation.

In 1 Corinthians 6:9-11 both the active and passive member in the homosexual encounter are mentioned.[26] Practicing homosexuals are included among the unrighteous who will not inherit the kingdom of God. It assumes such behavior can be ended ("And this is what some of you used to be"). In 1 Timothy 1:9-11 such are listed as among the lawless and disobedient. This comes in a list that is an updated version of the Ten Commandments. The parallel to the seventh commandment, which refers to adultery, is expanded to include immoral persons *(pornoi)* and sodomites *(arsenokoitai)*. The point is that all sexual intercourse outside of heterosexual marriage is considered banned by the Ten Commandments.

In brief, Paul uses creation and the moral law as well as God's sovereign will to ban homosexual conduct and warn of the dire spiritual danger this (along with heterosexual misconduct) produces. There is no question that Paul intended to eliminate such conduct in the Christian community, even while not cutting Christians off from homosexuals any more than from adulterers or others his mission sent them to.

The fourth reference is found in Jude 7 *(2 Peter 2:6)*. It uses Sodom and Gomorrah as examples of people who engaged in unnatural lust and found themselves experiencing the judgment of God. If I am correct in my earlier exegesis of the Jerusalem council, then that too bans homosexual conduct along with the other sexual practices listed in Leviticus 18. This would give us a fifth, though less direct, reference.

The early church fathers follow this consistent viewpoint. Charles Talbert again supplies a brief summary:

> Among the early Christian fathers two things may be noted. First, the apologists criticize Greco-Roman homosexuality (Aristides *Apology* 17 refers to both male and female activity; Justin 1 *Apology* 21, 25, 29; Athenagoras *A Plea for the Christians* 34; Clement of Alexandria *Exhortation to the Heathen* 2 claims that the pagan gods in their immorality did

not abstain even from homosexuality). Second, there is a very similar note to that already sounded in the Old Testament, ancient Judaism, and the New Testament. The Didache says, "You shall not murder, you shall not commit adultery, you shall not corrupt boys" *(2.1-2a)*. Polycarp asserts that those given to unnatural vice will not share in God's kingdom *(To the Philippians 5.3)*. Justin opposes exposing infants because most are reared for immoral purposes, including sodomy *(1 Apology 27, 36)*. The Apocalypse of Peter's vision of hell includes both male and female homosexuals. Clement of Alexandria says the sodomites burned with insane love for boys, so the city was destroyed *(Instructor 3.8)*. Similar attitudes are found in Tertullian, the *Apostolic Constitutions,* Chrysostom, Basil, and Augustine (D. S. Bailey, *Homosexuality and the Western Christian Tradition* [London: Longmans, Green & Co., 1955]; Peter Coleman, *Christian Attitudes to Homosexuality* [London: SPCK, 1980]).[27]

Without attempting to be exhaustive, we can come to a clear conclusion that homosexual conduct is consistently considered by both Testaments and by Jewish and Christian exegesis alike to be unacceptable sexual behavior and therefore is to be banned. This is not to say that homosexuals are unacceptable people or condemned as persons. Nonetheless, given the condemnation of the sexual behavior, it is impossible to legitimate even the most "acceptable" scenario for homosexuality: gay and lesbian, committed, monogamous "marriage." Such a proposal violates the order of creation, the normative codes of both the Old Testament and the New Testament, and the consistent tradition of Judaism and Christianity from the first century to the present.

Some may seek to pit Scripture against Scripture, noting that Jesus says nothing directly about homosexuality. But silence is a double-edged sword in any case. He also says nothing directly about incest. Are we to suppose silence is approval? Or that his attitude on this matter differed from that of the Old Testament, which he consistently cites as authoritative and whose misinterpreters he condemns because they substitute human tradition for the clear counsel of Scripture? Equally difficult to believe is that his brother James *(see Acts 15)*, as well as the whole apostolic church, went in a direction that he would have disapproved. The more likely scenario is that his silence here is a silence of approval of what no one misunderstood nor misinterpreted in his context (unlike the issues of purity, law, and wealth).

Conclusion

This negative conclusion cannot be left simply as a brute "no" in a context where the biblical position is too often joined with the rhetoric of homophobic polemic. There is far more than simply the condemnation of homosexual conduct in Scripture. God's action and purpose is on the mission of restoring all of creation to its intended design. Scripture offers God's loving intention for all human beings—heterosexuals, bisexuals, and homosexuals.

In our day the more serious issue (in the overall tally of sexual sin) is the sin of heterosexuals. At the current time the number of those infected with AIDS by sexual contact is overwhelmingly due to heterosexual intercourse. The vast majority of rapes and most incest and molestation of children are the result of heterosexual lust and perversion. The church needs to be sure there is balance and justice in its language about sexual sin and fairness in characterizing those gays and lesbians who are responsible, ethical, caring individuals in their civil and vocational lives.

Nonetheless, if and when the church is asked to validate and legitimate gay and lesbian sexual behavior in its most "acceptable" form (bonded, loving, lifelong monogamous "marriage"), it is being faithful to the covenant God of the Bible by saying a gentle but firm "no." While there are many practices that are less than ideal but not sinful, this is not one of them. In the midst of all the diverse marriage and family forms found in the Bible, forms at least tolerated if not approved, homosexual marriage and family is not among them. Because of the language used to speak about homosexual activity, it can never be among them.

The endogamous community multigenerational family is marked by (1) equality between brothers established by inheritance rules; (2) cohabitation of married sons with their parents; and (3) preferential and frequent marriage between the children of brothers.

The absolute nuclear family as found in the United States is marked by (1) no precise inheritance rules with the frequent use of wills to distribute the estate according to the will of the testator; (2) almost no cohabitation of married children with their parents; and (3) no marriage between the children of brothers.

2/
Will Our Daughters Have Faith? Gender Issues in the Local Congregation

Roberta Hestenes

THE DISREGARD AND NEGLECT of changing realities and challenges faced by many contemporary women continue to be serious barriers to effective evangelism and discipleship among those whom I will call "daughters of the church," those women whose Christian mothers were usually more or less "traditional" and were committed to serious involvement in the life and work of a local congregation. The local church must act justly toward all women and must actively strive to be a community of mutual love and respect. For our daughters to have faith, the church must witness to the love of Jesus Christ for all people, women and men, poor and affluent, young and old. The church must model compassion and integrity in its own life as a provisional sign of the kingdom to attract and hold its young women.

Women and the Church in the American Culture

"Where are the role models today for young, sharp Christian women who are well-educated and working professionally outside of the home?" The questioner was a young male Harvard Law School

graduate who had come to know and appreciate many of the
Christian women he had worked with while serving as an attorney
with the United States Justice Department.[1] He became aware of
large numbers of Christian women, single and married, in governmental offices who were well educated and well connected in a wide
variety of demanding professional roles. He also became aware that
very few of these women could identify significant female Christian
role models to inspire them in their own spiritual journeys of faith
and service. In addition, many women expressed discouragement at
the lack of interest and support they experienced as nontraditional
women in their local churches as well as at the ambivalence
expressed by Christians toward visibly competent professional
Christian women. These are not radical or strident women, but serious Christians feeling disconnected, discounted, or disregarded in
their churches.

Indicators of Change
The last twenty-five years in American culture have seen a remarkably
widespread transformation of assumptions and practices concerning
opportunities for women to participate equally alongside men in all
arenas of public life. This includes the significant opening of opportunities for women to assume leadership roles within Christian congregations, parishes, and institutions. Signs of positive progress
include significant increases in the number of women in theological
education, in some cases comprising over 50 percent of the student
population; the presence of women in most major Protestant denominational and seminary structures; the increased numbers of Christian
women faculty and administrators in Christian colleges and universities; the large numbers of ordained women now serving in specialized
and parish ministries;[2] and the significant and creative biblical, theological, and interdisciplinary work being done by Christian women
scholars themselves, thus contributing to an enriched tapestry of
scholarly ferment and reflection.

These indicators are augmented by an increasing number of male
biblical scholars and pastors, even in traditionally conservative and
evangelical seminaries and churches, who support, at least in theory,

full equality and opportunities for Christian women to use all of their gifts and abilities in the life of the church. This seems to suggest that there has been major progress on the path toward full partnership between women and men in the Christian community and as Christian participants in the larger society.

In spite of these signs, however, at many levels, most especially at the level of the local congregation, in hundreds of thousands of individual churches, the signals are much more mixed. While some progress has been made, the battle for full partnership between women and men as "co-workers" in the gospel *(see Philippians 4:1-6; cf. Romans 16),* whether lay or ordained, is far from won. In all too many churches, cultural and/or theological traditionalism seriously restricts the opportunities for Christian growth and service for women. On the other end of the spectrum more radically post-Christian "reimagining" efforts attack classical orthodox Christianity as antiwoman. While no church formally denies the dignity and worth of women, many local churches functionally minimize, ignore, or restrict the activities of young girls and women in their midst. Consequently, particularly in younger women with many options before them, congregations risk their turning away from the church as an important location for encouragement and for investing their abilities and spiritual gifts, time, and energy in a personally challenging and significant way. They may even turn away from Jesus Christ.

Where women were once restricted in their opportunities to work in the larger culture and so often turned to the church by serving as volunteers in the church school and women's association, ever increasing numbers of women are now working outside the home. Ironically, they may find more opportunities to be taken seriously there than they do in their local church. While work outside the home presents its own challenges and pressures, these new patterns present new challenges to the church as well.

The Risks of Prejudice

If the church does not understand these changes or neglects to take them seriously, it may fail to affirm or help women in their increasingly complex roles. It may embrace only one kind of woman, the traditional stay-at-home wife and mother, and subtly or explicitly reject the new majority of women who work outside the home. It may refuse to open opportunities for leadership gifts to be used within the church, thus turning many women away from the church to places where they feel more welcomed as active decision-makers. It may discourage the discovery and use of leadership abilities among young women. As young girls and university students notice the absence of Christian nontraditional female role models, they may even come to believe that Christianity itself is prejudiced against women. The church risks losing those women and losing their contributions to enabling the Christian community to live as a sign of the kingdom of God[3] in a lost, confused, and suffering world.

While Christian women in the workplace can and should have an important ministry as "salt" and "light" in their work, their gifts are needed in all manifestations of the church. They are needed in congregations and parachurch ministries, as volunteers or paid workers, as agents of love and reconciliation working with fellow Christians to demonstrate and declare the loving grace and mercy of God. In a static, unchanging context of conservatism and tradition, this might not present the challenge that it does in our constantly changing contemporary context. Our daughters, and sons, are not growing up in sheltered cloisters with limited options, but in a maelstrom of cultural turbulence. The Christian response must be biblically faithful and proactively just for all of its members. The church cannot remain captive to sub-biblical traditions and act in spiritually restrictive ways to any in its midst, young or old, female or male.

These issues are not best understood as a "male conspiracy" with women as "oppressed victims." This is far too simplistic and unhelpful. Both women and men are made in the image of God, and neither gender is free from sin. Christian women as well as men struggle with their history, biology, and psychology;[4] biblical understanding; differing contexts and perspectives; and the seductive siren calls of a self-centered consumer culture that can disguise destructive patterns and ways of living under attractive slogans of politics, economics, psychology, and even "post-Christian" extreme feminism.

Justice

The wounds of injustice, indifference, contention, and conflict still scar many women today and raise serious questions about justice and

Christian witness. These issues not only have an impact on Christian witness in the larger secular culture that is increasingly open to women's contributions; it also impacts the daughters of the church who experience the tensions between old and new, differing opportunities and restrictions within the culture and within the church, and the temptations to alternate between naïve denial of any problems and discouragement or abandonment of serious Christian engagement.

A Personal Viewpoint

This essay is written from the perspective of one evangelical Christian woman who has worked in Christian congregations and educational institutions for thirty-five years throughout this time of ferment. As a young woman, I worked part time with no formal credentials on a church staff. I received a very low salary without benefits, and I experienced constant insecurity about whether I would be allowed to continue working at all in a church whose lay leadership and ordained clergy were all male. As a theological educator working with thousands of male and female students over fifteen years, I witnessed the first explosion of women into theological education in the mid '70s. At first, the theological institution at which I taught was ill prepared and often openly hostile to encouraging the dreams of ministry for the women in its midst. This hostility seldom came from faculty but was common in the student body. It was an exciting time as professors and students alike were stretched to reconsider long-held views, and many rose to the challenge. I learned there, very early, that toleration of women's presence and the taking of their tuition dollars is not the same thing as advocacy, encouragement, or proactive justice for women. I have tracked the careers of many of these pioneering women students and clergy couples, often with great joy but also, alas too often, with sorrow and even anger at the burdens they have had to bear with little support.

Women in the Local Congregation

Serious Implications

While the numbers and roles of American women in the workplace have significantly expanded over the last twenty-five years, many local congregations often seem like the last ones to recognize the seriousness and implications of these changes for their own congregations and the women in their midst. Some denominations and congregations have made very determined efforts to take women seriously as partners in the gospel. Many have not.[5] This seems to be especially true in churches that identify themselves as "fundamentalist," "conservative," or "evangelical" in their theological orientation.[6] Women, and the men who care about them, often feel like they are known and treated in very different ways depending on where they are.

In the workplace, even with its salary disparities and glass ceilings, more and more women find themselves respected and valued contributors who are encouraged to bring all of their education, experience, and abilities to the table for the good of the whole enterprise. In all too many churches these same women can find themselves ignored, devalued, and demeaned as those needing to be highly controlled in where and how they can serve. Many Christian women simply adapt to the prevailing culture of the church. Others are deeply saddened, hurt, or even angered that their gifts and abilities are not allowed full expression in their church. Some find the gap between their experience of themselves as loved by God yet devalued by the church too great to bridge, and they drop out. Sometimes it is not only church that is dropped. With unanswered questions and painful experiences, they may be tempted to give up on Christian faith altogether or to become "post-Christian," moving beyond the orthodoxy of Christian belief to something more apparently helpful. All too often the church does not even notice when they are gone.

For many reasons, including the demands of employment, these daughters are seldom centered in church activities as their mothers were. Often the problem is simply one of time, trying to juggle busy lives full of conflicting demands. Family and home continue to be very important to most, yet the hours in a day are limited, and it is hard to "get it all done." The church may seem to provide one more guilt trip in a world where, for many women, guilt seems to come with the territory no matter what they do. Less traditional daughters may continue to appreciate some of what the church offers but find the themes, programs, and emphases of the congregation irrelevant, if not downright hostile, to the realities of their daily lives. And some, including those who have been exposed to more radically feminist theologies and perspectives, experience the church's silence, conservatism, or indifference as oppressive and harmful. Sometimes they actually experience the church as an obstacle to their own spiritual growth, a place to be avoided rather than embraced.[7] This is an unnecessary tragedy.

From the incredible variety of human possibilities, a few alternative scripts seem to compete for attention and allegiance as if there were only a very few ways in which a Christian woman could discern and follow God's calling in her life. Safe and helpful opportunities need to be provided for both younger and older women to sort out the various voices from which they are under constant bombardment. The church should be equipping and encouraging women to explore all the possibilities of fulfilling their potential as those loved by God.

Fully realized freedom and partnership between women and men, in which both genders seek to live out their faith holistically in all spheres of life is a necessary, although difficult, response to the gospel. There is little evidence at the beginning of this new millennium that the church recognizes this changing time of opportunity in the culture for women as the kairos moment that it could be for the church.

Biblical Foundations

I write from a theological perspective that believes in the full equality and partnership of women and men in marriage, family, church, and society. As a person committed to the full inspiration and authority of the Scriptures, I believe the Bible teaches that this partnership was always meant to be present. It was present in creation, broken by the fall, and restored by the incarnation, cross, and resurrection of Jesus Christ. Finally, it was demonstrated by the pouring out of the Holy Spirit on both women and men at Pentecost.[8] Careful studies in church history prove that the earliest church modeled what has been called "a radical discipleship of equals."[9] Ever since the Quakers and the radical Reformation, the church has been in an agonizingly slow but significant rediscovery of the importance of both women and men. While not denying the reality and significance of differences between men and women, these differences are no reason to deny the created worth, salvation, giftedness, and ministries of women alongside men. Paul's words forbidding some women from speaking out in ignorance or disturbing worship services were never intended to deny half of humanity its important place in the love and purpose of God. The gifts of the Spirit are given without consideration of gender. Each Christian is responsible to use the talents, gifts, and abilities given to her or him by God for the common good.

Gender Issues in American Churches

It is important to acknowledge the difficulties of discussing gender issues among any group of people. Gender is a pervasive reality that is inevitably viewed, and undoubtedly distorted, from within a person's own particular consciousness and context.

While significant conflict may appear less visible in most Protestant mainline and holiness denominations in which women may serve in all roles and offices, there still is a large gap between the rhetoric at "the top" and the reality at the local level. Patterns of discouragement of and discrimination against women as authoritative, credentialed, and significant leaders in local congregations persist. The polarization over these issues continues to be strong even in the midst of encouraging signs of change.

One helpful entry point to this incredibly complex subject is to focus on some of the particular gender issues in local congregations that are technically open to women as clergy, elders, and deacons. While the nuclear family continues to provide the first and most formative experiences and understandings of gender and meaning, local congregations are a significant location of formation and learning for millions of people throughout the life cycle.[10]

The Dynamics of Gender Assumptions

The dynamics of gender touch everything in the local congregation. Every congregation embodies certain assumptions about males and females, girls and boys, and how they ought to worship, study, and work apart or together. These can be healthy or unhealthy and everything in between. These dynamics are complex in individual families, and most churches can be understood as another level and larger scale of family structures, some functional and some dysfunctional, with an overlay of religious patterns and language. Because gender issues are so much a part of what we are and who we are, of our own sense of identity and security, they can stir up a lot of passion when they are challenged.

Unconscious Modeling

Usually there is little conscious awareness of what is being modeled, taught, or reinforced in the church on gender issues, whether for good or ill. Many people sincerely believe that there are no important gender issues in their church; anyone bringing them up is a troublemaker. Young college students and seminarians will dismiss the subject as unimportant, in part because it is so important that it is dangerous to discuss. One pastoral search committee preparing to call a woman pastor said that nobody cared about the gender of the pastor; it was a nonissue. Then the time came for the vote. Surprise! It was an issue for some after all. Until somebody proposes a change in the status quo of the roles of women alongside men, gender issues can be ignored by most people in the church. Both male and female pastors seldom preach on the topic. But once it comes up, awkward and painful conversations ensue, in part because invisible assumptions become visible.

Differences can be hard to discuss, much less resolve. One church nominating committee proposed for the first time a woman to serve on the deacon board. At the meeting at which the voting was to take place, one man stood and declared that "everyone knows that women can't handle money; you can't even trust them with a credit card." The audience laughed. The woman was voted down even though she was the senior vice president of a major bank where she was responsible for millions of dollars every day. She went home devastated that her church had rejected her willingness to serve without pay in an area of her giftedness. The question occurred to her, "If this is what the church believes about women, because I am a woman, is this what God believes about me?" She didn't find an answer easily.

Gender dynamics can be seen in such seemingly simple things as who is visible up front in worship and who is expected to work behind the scenes. Who ushers? On a staff with both men and women, who gets what size office? Does he get the corner and she get the Sunday school room? If the church is large, how are salaries determined? Who gets benefits? In one large church, all the male staff received medical and retirement benefits while none of the female staff did. Why?

Who teaches Sunday school and who goes to it? I was visiting a church in Kenya, Africa, and talking to the (male) pastor about the Sunday school. "Oh," he said, "that's for the children and the women." The boys and men don't go. Why not? Why do men run the church while women go to the Bible studies and small groups? Who runs the youth program, and how is success measured? What kind of activities are planned and by whom and for whom? One of the interesting dynamics in many congregations is the common shift from the female-centered church school to the male-centered youth programs back to the male pastor-centered adult church with a large majority of female members. Why? Who collects and counts the offering? Who makes the coffee and washes the communion cups? Who reads the Scripture? Who preaches? Why?

Most of these kinds of things "just happen" with little conscious awareness or discussion in most of our churches. "That is just the way we do things" or "We've always done it that way" often are offered as reasons that disguise deeply buried or unconscious assumptions about gender roles. In static societies where there is little change in roles, such limited awareness may not be much of a problem. In cultures like ours, which are experiencing enormous changes in understanding of the roles and abilities of women and men, such a lack of awareness may have damaging consequences even if unintended.

Assumptions about Responsibility in Marriage

Every congregation carries assumptions about who is mostly responsible for the success of marriage or who is at fault if there is sexual misconduct or physical abuse. Counseling sessions are seldom participated in equally by men and women. In one congregation, when it became known that the male senior pastor had carried on multiple sexual affairs with female members of the church staff, discussions focused on the seductiveness of the various women involved and the obvious failures of the pastor's wife. In this context the pastor was seen as the victim, the several women as serious sinners. In another church, the Christian education director was called in and fired when the pastor learned that her husband had filed for divorce. Because of the assumption that she was responsible for the continuance of their marriage, the husband's sexual behavior never came up. A youth director accused of sexual molestation by three different girls over a period of years was presumed to be the victim of slander. Gender assumptions were very much at work in these situations and yet were not named or available for cognitive discussion.

Issues of lay leadership, worship, education, finance, and administration are just a few of the dynamics that are related to gender in the local church.

One's Reality

In most churches people are not walking around with a sophisticated awareness of their own understandings about gender; they are simply living out of their reality. And it is not until someone or something breaks the silence or the status quo that the issues come to light. Very often a penalty is paid by the person who brings or tries to bring to consciousness the invisible, embedded assumptions. The hardest culture to analyze is the culture you inhabit. Like fish in water, we exist within our culture. The issue of gender is very often like the proverbial iceberg. The tip of the iceberg may be the subject under discussion, but the decision being wrestled with is only the tiniest part of the deeper realities that are influencing its resolution.

Emerging Challenges

While astonishing progress has been made over the last twenty-five years in the church's openness to women, we are still in the pioneering period. This assertion is controversial and subject to challenge, and it depends a lot on where you sit. Many seminary students seldom seem willing to talk about gender issues in marriage and ministry. Many say those are not "their" issues. The church cannot overcome two thousand years of church belief and practice in a few decades or even in a century of effort. I am personally encouraged by many of the changes I have seen but also extremely aware of what hasn't changed. Patience and endurance are needed for what is unlikely to change quickly.

A Culture of Change

Notice the interaction between our rapidly changing culture and an often conserving church seeking to be faithful to Christian tradition and teaching. We inhabit a culture of change, and by and large much of the church seeks to be a conserving institution. I have been in a number of churches whose theology would not be formally labeled as conservative, but whose culture is a culture of conserving traditions, habits, patterns, insights, and ways of thinking from the past. This can be a highly valued and appropriate function of the church. Yet complex tensions exist between movements in the culture and the conserving nature of the church.

Often people make major changes in their behavior while continuing to espouse their former understandings and values—meaning that people's behavior sometimes changes faster than their theology or their affirmation of what they believe is right or wrong. I was once conducting a retreat for three hundred women from a church that would be sociologically characterized as a lower-middle-class church. The women in that retreat almost to the last one affirmed a traditional hierarchy of roles for men and women in marriage and in the church. They were very traditional in how they expressed what they believed was right or wrong about those matters. But when I began to probe about how they actually lived their lives, those women had been involved in changing the dynamics of their marital relationships in profound ways. Their behavior was way out of sync with the language they used to describe what they believed, yet they didn't appear conflicted. They were inconsistent. They were living their lives in the new realities but using the old ways of thinking as a way of making sense out of their lives. Some of the things, for instance, that psychologists have discovered—like the shift in marital power when a woman makes more income than her husband—were actually true for these women. Still, they were defending the traditional power dynamics between husbands and wives. What people say may not reflect how they are living.

Grace toward Others

We must be very careful about stereotyping good people and bad people, friends and enemies, on the basis of gender beliefs. I began learning a long time ago not to demonize people who are in a different place than I am. Do not turn such people into enemies in your mind or actions. If they turn themselves into your enemies, so be it. But do not assume that any other is automatically the enemy. In a local congregation, that is absolutely crucial, because you will blow the local congregation apart if you start demonizing everyone there who doesn't say things the way you do, understand things the way you do, or want the same amount of change in the same amount of time as you do. A local congregation is made up of a complicated mix of real people trying to live their lives in a messy world.

Revisiting American Church Culture

It is well known that a gap exists between national denominational rules and the practices of local churches. You particularly know this if you are in a mainline denomination. For example, the American Baptist Church has been supportive of women in ordained formal leadership in their churches for many, many years. Yet I found when I became the female president of an American Baptist College that I received most invitations to speak in American Baptist Churches on Mother's Day and Women's Sundays. The culture was way out of sync at the local congregational level from policy at the national level. This difference can set up a gap for seminarians, because the seminary very often will focus on what is desirable or what is official. Still, reality in a local church may be very different. The distance between the denomination and the local congregation can be enormous.

One difference is the lack of a career track or "ladder" for women employed by the church. Even more serious is the problem of the "second or third job" for trained women clergy. It is what I call the "all dressed up and no place to go" phenomenon, in which women get an entry-level job and maybe a second job in a congregation and then have no place to go but sideways. In other words, there are very few women in senior pastorates in multiple staff churches or at the top of parachurch or denominational structures. This is beginning to change in a few places, but very slowly.

What roles are open in terms of the pastorate? They are mostly as an assistant or associate or as solo clergy in churches of less than 150 people. Are some churches open to women in all roles except as senior pastor? Perhaps that is because in many local congregations we have come to the point where many are allowed to function as daughters and sisters in the congregations—as assistants and associates in pastoral roles. But there is a lot of ambivalence about women moving into solo or senior leadership. I think that is because, at a deep psychological level, the image of the patriarchal, traditional family shapes our understanding of biblical metaphors about the church as family or the household of God. The family is a common biblical image. People apply their images of family to the church. This has been done with relatively minor discomfort in all kinds of churches where women are added to a staff. They are the second or third or fourth person on the team. As long as women are perceived as helping someone male in a leadership role, they are acceptable. It is when women begin to cross that image of family—the traditional model of family in which the father is the head of the family and mother is doing whatever—that people begin to get uncomfortable. The discomfort is felt because the models are out of sync and psychologically difficult for people to experience. Resistance to change here is stubborn.

Because of these and other political, pastoral, and theological problems, there are many hundreds, if not thousands, of women who choose not to use the historic label "evangelical" as a self-descriptor. They have not lost the faith nor have they necessarily left the church, but they do not identify emotionally or theologically with evangelicalism as a movement. There are a number of reasons, one of which is the lack of welcome, affirmation, and encouragement for women within the evangelical movement at all levels. I consider this a great loss.

Fairness in Congregations

Are salary, benefits, and working conditions fair and comparable to those of men at the same level? A woman close to me had finished seminary and interviewed. She asked if she would have an office, and a selection committee member took her to a closet and said the church could clean it out. This closet had no air circulation or windows, but the committee members thought they could get a small desk into the closet. She asked how many of the men on the staff in comparable positions were in closets. None of them were. She is not in the ministry today. She didn't believe the church would take her seriously. Unfortunately, she was probably right. Some would presume she should just accept what she was offered. If she was not happy about it, she had a spiritual problem. But this was not a spiritual problem; it was a justice problem. If a woman asks about her salary, many think she is not spiritual. If she asks about benefits, she is self-centered. Issues of fairness in congregations are very serious issues of justice that must not be left only to the women directly impacted.

In our congregations, one of the things that holds some women back is fear. There are a lot of different reasons for fear, including paranoia that people are out to get you. Sometimes in the best of churches there may be people out to get you. But there will also be many others who support and encourage. Congregations are made up of ordinary human beings. Some of them are healthy, and some of them are not healthy. Some of them will support and encourage women, and others will do women damage. So through each woman's own spiritual journey, through participation in Christian community, through a life of prayer and Scripture reading, women have to find the courage to overcome fear of criticism or fear of failure.

Language

People care a lot about language, and messing with their hymns is a good way to rapidly alienate people in the local congregation. People care less about the woman issue than they care about your messing with their favorite hymns. The language in which we say or sing our faith is close to the bone. Care, patience, tact, and timing should help form the strategy toward using more inclusive language in music and worship. I strongly suggest using overheads, bulletins, hymnals, and prayers that use inclusive language for the people of God. It matters to our daughters.

Conclusions

While the mystery of personal faith in Christ lies within the province of the Holy Spirit, there are some things churches can do to encourage our daughters.

- Preach, teach, and encourage an understanding of Scripture that affirms the worth and equality of women and men in creation, in redemption, in Christian community, and in Christian ministry.
- Do everything possible to build and strengthen Christian marriages in which wives and husbands are mutually submissive to Christ and to each other in love and faithfulness. Do this through pre- and postmarital counseling, seminars and retreats, adult education on biblical perspectives on marriage, classes on communication and conflict resolution skills, and "couples' nights out" with baby-sitting provided. When parents model mutual

respect, service, and love within committed Christian marriages, they give a powerful witness to Jesus Christ.

- Regularly provide good printed material and role models of gifted Christian women for young girls, teenagers, and students in Sunday school programs, in worship, and in decision-making settings in the community.
- Encourage the development and use of all spiritual gifts by women, including in preaching, teaching, and worship leadership as well as in justice and in outreach ministries.
- Develop an environment of small covenant groups for women, single and married, for friendship and support, study, prayer, and action.
- Provide inclusive-language translations of Scriptures, hymns, and corporate prayer. Also provide a good library of helpful books on biblical, theological, and practical issues related to partnership between women and men.[11]
- Provide for staff fairness in salaries and working conditions. Develop processes to handle issues of abuse, sexual harassment, and perceived injustice.
- Pray specifically for girls, youth, and women along with men for God's love and power to be released in their lives.

A church committed to these acts of love and justice provides a healthy environment where our daughters can find faith and grow in it.

BIBLIOGRAPHY

Balswick, Jack, and Judith Balswick. *The Dual Earner Marriage: The Elaborate Balancing Act.* Grand Rapids: Revell, 1992.

Barton, Ruth H. *Becoming a Woman of Strength: 14 Life Challenges for Women.* Wheaton, Ill.: Harold Shaw, 1999.

—. *Equal to the Task: Men and Women in Partnership.* Downers Grove, Ill.: InterVarsity Press, 1998.

Becker, Carol E. *Leading Women: How Church Women Can Avoid Leadership Traps and Negotiate the Gender Maze.* Nashville: Abingdon, 1996.

Bilezikian, Gilbert G. *Beyond Sex Roles: What the Bible Says about a Woman's Place in Church and Family.* 2d ed. Grand Rapids: Baker, 1986.

—. *Community 101: Reclaiming the Local Church as Community of Oneness.*

Grand Rapids: Zondervan, 1997.

Carroll, Jackson W., Barbara Hargrove, and Adair T. Lummis. *Women of the Cloth: A New Opportunity for Churches.* New York: Harper and Row, 1983.

Conway, Jim, and Sally Conway. *Sexual Harassment No More.* Downers Grove, Ill.: InterVarsity Press, 1993.

Grenz, Stanley J., and Denise M. Kjesbo. *Women in the Church: A Biblical Theology of Women in Ministry.* Downers Grove, Ill.: InterVarsity Press, 1995.

Groothuis, Rebecca M. *Women Caught in the Conflict: The Culture War between Traditionalism and Feminism.* Eugene, Ore.: Wipf & Stock Publishers, 1994.

Keener, Craig S. *Paul, Women and Wives: Marriage and Women's Ministry in the Letters of Paul.* Peabody, Mass.: Hendrickson, 1992.

Sanders, Cheryl J. *Ministry at the Margins: The Prophetic Ministry of Women, Youth and the Poor.* Downers Grove, Ill.: InterVarsity Press, 1997.

Strauss, Mark L. *Distorting Scripture? The Challenge of Bible Translation and Gender Accuracy.* Downers Grove, Ill.: InterVarsity Press, 1998.

Tucker, Ruth A., and Walter Liefeld. *Daughters of the Churches: Women and Ministry from New Testament Times to the Present.* Grand Rapids: Zondervan, 1987.

Van Leeuwen, Mary S. *Gender and Grace: Love, Work, and Parenting in a Changing World.* Downers Grove, Ill.: InterVarsity Press, 1990.

Van Leeuwen, Mary S., and Annelies Knoppers. *After Eden: Facing the Challenge of Gender Reconciliation.* Grand Rapids: Eerdmans, 1993.

Zikmund, Barbara B., Adair T. Lummis, and Patricia M. Y. Chang. *Clergy Women: An Uphill Calling.* Louisville: Westminster John Knox, 1998.

3/
Inclusive Language and the Means of Grace

Gretchen Gaebelein Hull

THE OCTOBER 1999 ISSUE of *National Geographic* included a sky chart in which an arrow pointing to a tiny spot representing our solar system announced: "We are here." Such a graphic depiction of earth's corner of the universe illustrates the Book of Job's observation that God "stretches out the north over the void, and hangs the earth upon nothing" *(26:7, RSV)*. It also reminds us that, from a cosmic perspective, Shakespeare was on target in terming humanity "this quintessence of dust."[1] Seeing ourselves situated amid the vastness of space, we can only humbly echo the psalmist's words:

> O LORD, our Sovereign,
> > how majestic is your name in all the earth!...
> When I look at your heavens, the work of your fingers,
> > the moon and the stars that you have established;
> what are human beings that you are mindful of them,
> > mortals that you care for them?
> > > —*Psalm 8:1,3-4*

Yet the remarkable message of the Bible is that our Creator is not aloof from us, but chooses to be self-revealing. God's gracious self-revelation is made known through the intricate marvels of creation (the Designer revealed in the design; see *Psalm 19:1-4; Romans 1:19-20*); God speaks verbally as well. A. W. Tozer said of this phenomenon: "That God is here and that he is speaking—these truths are back of all other Bible truths; without them there could be no revelation at all." [2]

That the infinite God condescends to speak with finite humanity is compelling evidence of God's interest in human life, but that God continually speaks in order to offer us a personal relationship ("I will be your God and you will be my people") is the deepest indication of God's love and concern. From the first words spoken to the man and the woman in the Garden of Eden, God has reached out to us humans in all our frailty and—even when we stray—has offered us new life and renewed fellowship by means of various covenantal initiatives that are based solely on God's grace and not on human merit *(Ephesians 2:1-10)*.[3] The climax of God's loving self-revelation is that "the Word became flesh and lived among us...full of grace and truth" *(John 1:14),* and it is the Living Word himself who makes plain the ultimate purpose of such condescension: "The Son of Man came to seek out and to save the lost," and "I came that they may have life, and have it abundantly" *(Luke 19:10; John 10:10).*

Scripture As a Means of Grace

Oswald Chambers observed, "The Bible is not a book containing communications from God, it is God's revelation of Himself in the limitation of words."[4] The written Word is therefore not only a record of God's acts of saving grace; but the reading, preaching, teaching, and hearing of Scripture are important means by which that grace continues to be imparted to us today. As Richard Foster points out, "We come to Scripture to be changed, not to amass information....We want life-transforming truth, not just good feelings."[5]

But once transformed into "new creations" (see *2 Corinthians 5:17*), we continue to look to the inspired Scriptures to guide us in our walk of faith. The Word that first instructed us about salvation now teaches, reproves, corrects, and trains us *(2 Timothy 3:14-17)* to the end that we "grow in the grace and knowledge of our Lord and Savior Jesus Christ" *(2 Peter 3:18)*. Frank Gaebelein concluded, "Daily reading of the Word of God is beyond question a continuing means of grace for untold multitudes of God's people."[6] Of course, it is Jesus himself who has already called us into such an ongoing personal and corporate endeavor, promising: "If you continue in my word, you are truly my disciples; and you will know the truth, and the truth will make you free" *(John 8:31-32)*.

Jesus also commands his disciples to proclaim the Good News to those who have not yet heard so that others may have opportunity to experience God's grace for themselves. Jesus' Great Commission *(Matthew 28:19-20)* and his subsequent declaration that his disciples will witness "to the ends of the earth" *(Acts 1:8)* presuppose that the gospel will be presented to every people group. At Pentecost the Holy Spirit miraculously enabled Jesus' followers to speak to a diverse audience in their native languages *(Acts 2:7)*, with the result that those hearing this inspired speech marveled that "in our own languages we hear them speaking about God's deeds of power" *(v. 11)*.

These texts make it abundantly clear that God wants God's divine Word to be accessible. Therefore, the purpose of Bible translation is that each individual may hear God's Word proclaimed in his or her own language. From the first translation of the Hebrew Scriptures into Greek, then the Greek into Latin, and right down to the present day, translators have sought to craft versions that enable people to read Scripture in their own native tongues, with no linguistic barriers hindering transmission of God's gracious words of life.

Translation Challenges

Although the translator's goal is to make the donor languages (Hebrew and Greek) accurately understood in the receptor language (English), it quickly becomes apparent even to the layperson that reaching this goal is far from easy. Languages are not exact images of each other, as a quick examination of an Interlinear Hebrew-English Old Testament or Interlinear Greek-English New Testament demonstrates.[7]

Even the person most dedicated to "formal" equivalency (popularly termed "literal" translation) will have to depart from a rigid word-for-word rendition of the Hebrew or Greek, because, as Mark Strauss notes, "An overly literal approach can contribute to misunderstanding of the biblical text."[8] Since the original Scriptures were inspired ("God-breathed," *2 Timothy 3:16*), many contemporary translation teams avoid such wooden literalism and seek to produce Bible versions that also "breathe" in the receptor language—versions exhibiting "functional" or "dynamic" equivalency.

Producing any translation involves far more than knowing the meaning of words and the grammatical rules governing the use of those words, in either the donor or receptor language. As John Kohlenberger explains, "There is no such thing as the literal meaning of a word. Words have to be translated contextually in order to be accurate."[9] Because a particular language reflects the characteristic manner of verbal communication for an individual people group, the translator's knowledge of cultural and idiomatic usage will also affect proper word selection and sentence structure. Commenting on his efforts for the Wycliffe Bible Translators working in Papua New Guinea, Robin Thurman observed: "You have to work hard to make your translation fit the culture as well as the language. A wrong translation can lead to some really funny beliefs."[10]

But in addition, when working with the receptor language the translator must take into account the fact that any spoken language changes. Unlike classical Greek and Latin, for example, which are fixed in ancient historical settings and thus termed dead languages, a living language such as English undergoes continual modifications. Even a cursory examination of the fourteenth-century Wycliffe Version, the sixteenth-century King James Version, and a twentieth-century version such as The New Living Translation shows the dramatic development of the English language. The result, as Donald Carson states, is that "[a]ll translations are temporary. This is because the receptor language changes; there are no exceptions."[11] Recognizing this fact, back in 1978 a pamphlet introducing the popular New International Version noted that the translator's work is never done. In answer to the question "Will there be further revisions of the NIV?" the printed response was:

> Yes and no. Basically no. There will be no wholesale changes. Yet as time goes on, three things will happen:

1. More ancient manuscripts will be found...that may affect the underlying Hebrew or Greek text.

2. New linguistic insights into the ancient languages will clarify presently obscure words and idioms.

3. English words will change their meanings.[12]

A Significant Shift

In the United States of America, as in many other English-speaking nations, one contemporary linguistic change has been the move toward using inclusive language—employing words and phrases that clearly include everyone when the intent is to exclude no one. The most obvious example of inclusive language has been the abandonment of the masculine-oriented generic usage *(mankind, man, men, he, him)* when the intent is to refer to all human beings, and using inclusive words instead *(humanity, humankind, human beings, they, he or she)*.

People who resist this shift may cite the wording of the 1776 Declaration of Independence: "We hold these truths to be self-evident, that all men are created equal, that they are endowed by their Creator with certain unalienable rights." Such traditionalists say, "If the generic *men* was good enough for the nation's founders, it should be good enough for us today." These persons have forgotten that while theoretically "all men" included every person equally, and while Thomas Paine wrote contemporaneously of *The Rights of Man,* nevertheless, the eighteenth-century reality was that "unalienable rights" of "all men" did not extend to the black slave population, Native Americans, or to women. Actual constitutional amendments were eventually required to secure equal citizenship status for minorities. Furthermore, in both the United States and England, women did not receive the vote until the twentieth century, and in many instances women and minorities are still looking for equal protection under the law.

Sad but true, masculine generic English usage has not always included all human beings. Recognizing this problem, persons concerned with ending discrimination against women and minorities have begun using inclusive language. When the United Nations' landmark Universal Declaration of Human Rights was adopted in 1948 as the agreed-upon international standard for justice issues, no one suggested calling it the Universal Declaration of the Rights of Man.

In recent decades there has also been a noticeable shift away from any notion that "Man is the measure of all things," for here again severe inequities have become apparent. In former years, all-male juries might have been asked to decide what a "reasonable man" would conclude about a certain matter, but Americans now see the injustice of such an approach. We are painfully aware that this "reasonable man" standard did not include all males, for we look back with shame upon the harm inflicted upon our black brothers by the decisions of biased all-white male juries (and legislatures as well). All too frequently what the "reasonable" white man decided should be appropriate policy was in reality a discriminatory device, not an inclusive standard. Furthermore, what men in general legislated was not always in the best interests of women either. But with racial and ethnic minorities and women now recognized as equal citizens with white men, the fairer question becomes: "What would a reasonable *person* conclude?"

Accuracy and Courtesy

A further refinement of inclusive-language usage has been the move toward gender accuracy—careful wording that indicates all human beings if the intent is to include women as well as men but that is unmistakably gender specific when only one sex is meant. This is a much-needed change.

For example, if I see an advertisement for a "Laymen's Conference," I (as a woman) will have to discover whether or not my participation is welcome. Obviously it is appropriate to have an all-male conference, just as it is appropriate to organize an all-female conference. But using the masculine-oriented "Laymen" requires me to find an interpreter to tell me if the organizers mean their wording generically or specifically. If the meaning is indeed generic, using "Laypeople's Conference" or even "Lay Conference" would be more helpful.

Traditionalist males have not always appreciated this need for interpreting the masculine English generic, for they will always feel included however the word *man* is used. But as long as the male-oriented usage is retained, women will always have to check to see whether or not females are in fact welcome. As a female denominational leader explained back in 1984: "In reading the Gospel, women shouldn't have to decide, either consciously or unconsciously, whether they are included."[13]

In contemporary social and academic discourse, using *human beings* instead of *men* when the intent is inclusive does not represent caving in to some supposed political correctness or feminist pressure, but is simply a long-overdue move toward accuracy and courtesy. If Bible translations are to speak to contemporary readers, English versions must reflect this unmistakable shift.

Although persons unaware of language development, or older persons who remain comfortable with the masculinized generic because of its familiarity, may resist using either inclusive or gender-accurate language, Mark Strauss warns: "If generic masculines are on their way out in contemporary English, Bible translations must translate accordingly or become archaic, outdated and inaccurate."[14] And John Stott unequivocally declares, "When 'man' means human being, without any intention to exclude women…then to retain such gender-specific words would be offensive. Even worse, it would actually misrepresent the meaning of the text."[15]

The Biblical Evidence

However, more foundational than any linguistic or cultural shifts in the English-speaking world is that inclusive and gender-accurate wording is biblically faithful—faithful to the original generic Hebrew and Greek words, faithful to their use in the biblical context itself, and faithful to the intent of the biblical writers. Only a very short time studying basic research tools accessible to any interested open-minded person underscores the careful manner in which Scripture itself speaks of human beings.

Both *Strong's Exhaustive Concordance of the Bible* and *Young's Analytical Concordance of the Bible* define the relevant Hebrew *'ādām* and Greek *anthrōpos* as having the meaning of "human being" and list the many instances where these words are used generically in the biblical text. In addition, *A Greek-English Lexicon of the New*

Testament and Other Early Christian Literature by Arndt and Gingrich, as well as Vine's more popularly presented *An Expository Dictionary of New Testament Words,* also define *anthrōpos* as "human being" and present further contextual support for translations using "human being" as the appropriate English generic in place of the English word "man." These linguistic authorities support inclusive pronoun usage as well, such as translating the Greek word *tis* as "anyone." Both lexicons make clear the distinction between *anēr* (a person of the male sex and never used of a female) and *anthrōpos.* The plural of *anthrōpos* is rendered "people," with the pronoun usage being "you" or "everyone."

Modern English versions that reflect this biblical language can hardly be termed radical! In fact, as John Kohlenberger notes, "The use of gender-inclusive language in modern translations follows patterns established in the Greek Septuagint, the Greek New Testament, and historic English versions. It's not new, it's just more thorough in its application."[16]

The Language of Grace
The doctrine of common grace describes the blessings God chooses to bestow on all humanity, irrespective of individual merit, such as when God sends the rain to refresh all persons equally. The particular language form used by the New Testament writers demonstrates that grace, for the common *(koinē)* Greek they employed was the one language most readily understood throughout the ancient Mediterranean world. By this means, God insured that the written Word revealing the saving work of the Incarnate Word would be accessible to persons of diverse backgrounds and cultures, rich or poor, male or female, slave or free. In obedience to the Great Commission, the New Testament writers not only preserved Jesus' words but transmitted those words through the linguistic vehicle best suited to reach the widest possible audience with the good news that "the grace of God has appeared, bringing salvation to all" *(Titus 2:11).*

This accessible written Word then itself became a vital means through which people could receive God's special saving grace. As the apostle John explained, "[T]hese are written so that you may come to believe that Jesus is the Messiah, the Son of God, and that through believing you may have life in his name" *(John 20:31)*. Similarly with Bible translations down through the ages: these versions are also written so that subsequent generations worldwide might hear the Good News in their own tongues and might also come to believing faith in Jesus Christ as Lord and Savior.

The transmission of Scripture is an example of God's common grace; the words of Scripture present God's special grace in the person and work of Jesus Christ. Our English translations must emulate this New Testament pattern so that the Good News is readily accessible to all contemporary readers and can for them become a means of grace. As Mark Strauss has pointed out, "Just as God took on the form of common humanity when he revealed himself as the living Word, so his written Word was revealed in language that the person on the street could understand. This fact alone should convince us to translate Scripture into contemporary idiomatic English—not an imitation English that artificially mimics the pattern and structure of either Greek or Hebrew."[17]

Significantly, it is Jesus himself who points us away from preoccupation with gender and calls us to focus on discipleship, saying: "Blessed rather are those who hear the word of God and obey it!" *(Luke 11:28)*. Jesus also said, "If you love me, you will keep my commandments" *(John 14:15)*, activity that surely involves obedience to the Great Commission. Jesus' followers are commanded not only to "Go therefore and make disciples of all nations" but also to teach these newest disciples themselves to obey his words—words that Jesus himself had earlier declared to be "spirit and life" *(John 6:63)*, and thus words that for all new converts will now become a means of grace.

The Language of Redemption and Evangelism

Biblically faithful inclusive language not only most effectively transmits God's gracious offer of salvation *to* all human beings, but inclusive language most accurately represents the incarnate Lord's redemptive work as being efficacious *for* all who believe. This is especially welcome news to share with any women who feel distanced from Jesus Christ because he appears to them to be a Savior for men only. Aware that the English masculine generic usage does not always include females equally in secular society, these women have questioned how such usage can include them redemptively. They know that a debt that is not assumed cannot be redeemed, and when (as a result of certain English translations) Christ's male form appears to these women to be a key component of the Incarnation, they ask how a male can fully identify with a female or fully redeem a woman's sin.

In response, inclusive-language English Bible versions make plain that the wonder of the Incarnation is not that Christ took on the form of a male but that the Second Person of the Trinity condescended ("emptied himself") to become a *human* being *(Philippians 2:7).*[18] Therefore, Roger Nicole points out, "[P]eople of any human community could unmistakably recognize Jesus Christ as one of them, for the main thing he assumed is generic humanity, found alike in every member of the race, male or female, child or adult, great or small, Jew or Gentile."[19] The mediating work of Christ is accessible to all people, regardless of their circumstantial condition. The redemptive work of Christ is effective for all who believe, bringing them all into the one family of God. As Dietrich Bonhoeffer explained, "When God's Son took on flesh, he truly and bodily took on, out of pure grace, our being, our nature, ourselves....We belong to him because we are in him. That is why the Scriptures call us the Body of Christ."[20]

In Luke 5:10 Jesus metaphorically described evangelism as fishing for *people.*[21] In today's world, fulfilling our call to be fishers of men and women will mean welcoming Bible versions that draw all persons into the text, rather than perpetuating versions that distance women from God's gracious, redemptive words of life. Inclusive-language versions are a key evangelistic tool; only these versions make crystal clear that no woman need ever doubt her full inclusion in God's invitation to believe, no woman need ever doubt that Jesus is Redeemer for all who believe, and no woman need ever doubt that God will welcome her equally into the household of faith. What good news to proclaim!

Thus it is that not only from a secular, cultural point of view, or with the intent of reflecting modern English usage, but it is from a biblical, exegetical, theological, and missiological point of view that translations using biblically faithful inclusive and gender-accurate language best represent the gospel and most clearly transmit that gospel to English-speaking readers.

The Language of Community

Inclusive-language translations also speak directly to the deep human desire for full acceptance in the entire human family. God created us to be social beings *(Genesis 2:18-23),* and as such we establish individual families and also join together to form communities. Spiritually, our relational needs are met when through believing faith we become children of God *(John 1:12),* assured of dwelling in the household of the Lord forever *(Psalm 23:6; John 14:3).* Jesus frequently used the imagery of a celebratory banquet to describe this future joyous communal life, and he specifically promised that "people will come from east and west, from north and south, and will eat in the kingdom of God" *(Luke 13:29).*

Yet in this present world, as Henri Nouwen observed, "The contemporary society in which we find ourselves makes us acutely aware of our loneliness....In our world full of strangers, estranged from their own past, culture, and country, from their neighbors, friends, and family, from their deepest self and their God, we witness a painful search for a hospitable place where life can be lived without fear and where community can be found."[22] Sadly, although people yearn to find someone who will befriend them and empathize with them, one of the most frequent and poignant complaints is "You just don't understand me."

What a relief, therefore, to read in Scripture that our Creator God not only knows all about us, but that "God will satisfy every need of [ours] according to his riches in glory in Christ Jesus" *(Philippians 4:19)*—including our human need for acceptance and companionship. What a joy for the individual woman as well as for the individual man to have this need met now by being warmly welcomed into the priesthood of all believers. As Carl Henry succinctly put it, "The church of Jesus Christ is a community, not a clique."[23]

Traditionalists need not fear that, in its emphasis on community, inclusive-language usage will erode God-given gender distinctives. This is not a case of "either/or" but of "both/and." The Genesis account of our human origins *(1:26-28)* is itself both inclusive and gender-accurate, revealing our unique commonality as beings created "in the image of God" while celebrating the two distinct forms in which that commonality appears ("male and female he created them"). The New Testament metaphor of the one body of believers *(1 Corinthians 12:12-27)* also makes plain that distinctives are not erased within the new community, for the unique persons who comprise the whole each retain their own individuality and giftedness. Inclusive-language translations encourage each believer to use his or her gifts for the good of the one faith community by increasing our awareness that women as well as men are equal to serve their one Lord.

Furthermore, by eliminating any suggestion of preference for the masculine, using inclusive language for human beings prevents an un-Christlike competition between the sexes and fosters the unity for which Jesus prayed *(John 17:20-23)*. Inclusive language takes the emphasis off gender and centers our energies on our mutual call to be "good stewards of the manifold grace of God" *(1 Peter 4:10)*.

Dietrich Bonhoeffer sums up the interconnectedness of the One and the many as he declares, "Our community with one another consists solely in what Christ has done for both of us....I have community with others and I shall continue to have it only through Jesus Christ. The more genuine and deeper our community becomes, the more will everything else between us recede, the more clearly and purely will Jesus Christ and his work become the one and only thing that is vital between us. We have one another only through Christ, but through Christ we do have one another, wholly, and for all eternity."[24]

In a fallen world, fiercely competitive and increasingly suspicious of strangers, the good news is that Christians do not have to "go it alone" but receive friendship, support, and encouragement from the other members of the body of Christ. The full acceptance of each new child of God into God's family circle not only ends the individual's isolation but witnesses to an alienated world that in Christ all barriers to fellowship and community are removed, including culturally and linguistically based gender barriers. This is a message of grace that contemporary women and men alike need to hear, and this is a message that biblically faithful inclusive-language versions of Scripture most accurately present.[25]

4/
The Wounds of a Friend: A Critique of Traditional, Protestant, North American Youth Ministry at the End of the Millennium

Duffy Robbins

Faithful are the wounds of a friend,
but the kisses of an enemy are deceitful.
                    —*Proverbs 27:6, KJV*

ONE OF THE GREAT CONTRIBUTIONS Tony Campolo has made to the church over the last fifteen years has been his faithful, insightful (and it might be added, relentless) critique of the church's ministry to adolescents. There really have been no other writers who have examined modern youth ministry under the microscope of what Campolo calls "sociotheology,"[1] certainly not with the zeal and with the widespread hearing that Campolo has. As a prolific writer in youth ministry publications,[2] and as a regular speaker at the National Youth Workers Convention,[3] Dr. Campolo has been able to challenge, encourage, chide, provoke, instruct, and occasionally outrage (one of Campolo's "spiritual gifts") several thousand youth workers on an annual basis. This has allowed his commentary to remain topical and relevant. His is consistently one of the most respected voices bringing critique to this growing arena of the church.

It is in this spirit of the "faithful wounds" of a friend that this essay will attempt to identify several broad areas of concern related to traditional, Protestant, North American youth ministry[4] at the end of the millennium. The focus in this forum on negative factors is not to imply that the picture is all bad. It isn't. Indeed, implicit in some of these critical observations are positive statements. But the uncomfortable probe and the unflattering diagnosis may be the faithful wounds that awaken us to a problem. Campolo has shown us the value of the prophet's voice in the modern church. What follows are not the words of a prophet nor the "son of a prophet" *(cf. Amos 7:14)*. But what they are most surely are "the wounds of a friend."

"Tarzan Christianity"

As a young boy, one of my favorite television heroes was Tarzan, "King of the Jungle." I can still see him flying through forests, his bronzed muscles framed by that classic leopard-skin outfit, the whole jungle coming alive with the sound of his trademark scream.

The most amazing part of the Tarzan show was watching him swing from tree to tree. There was always a vine right where he needed it, always the right length, and always loose enough to release from the tree with the slightest tug. I used to wonder about that. I wandered in the woods behind our house looking up at the treetops, suspicious that it would take more than a quick pull to launch the vines I saw. I worried about what might happen if Tarzan's vine were ever too long or too short. I imagined how sad it would be to see my leopard-clad hero swing down into the jungle floor with a thud. Or how gruesome it might be if Tarzan were to just someday come to the edge of the jungle and simply run out of trees. Imagine Tarzan swinging through the jungle…first to one tree…then to another…then to another…then to another…when all of a sudden he comes to a clearing. No tree. No vine. Just a blur of flesh and leopard skin flying through the air. Not a pretty thought.

Yet it is precisely that image that might come to mind if we were to characterize much of the current practice of status quo youth ministry. We can almost imagine in our mind's eye a generation of the church's youth "swinging" from Sunday night to Sunday night, youth meeting to youth meeting, retreat to festival, summer camp to mission trip. Great excitement is in the air. More students are coming to church.[5] Youth programs are getting larger and gaining momentum.[6]

Yet there is cause for concern. What will happen to the youth when they come to "the clearing"? What will happen when they leave their youth groups and no longer have the luxury of swinging from one treetop experience to the next? What will happen when they find themselves out there in the jungle of everyday life with all of its risks and dangers? We must be cautioned that modern-day youth ministry is breeding students who are ripe for a classic case of "crash and burn"—a plunging, groping blur of leopard skin, Bible cover, Christian T-shirt, and WWJD bracelet. In short, we may be planting in our youth programs the seeds of "Tarzan Christianity."

Is There Life after Treetops?

To be sure, it is God who begins the "good work," and it is God who can see it through to "completion" *(Philippians 1:6)*. But youth workers must recognize that our task is not completed just by getting teenage Tarzans to jump into the jungle; we need to help them to land, and to stand, and to keep walking with Christ on a daily basis. The mission of effective youth ministry is not to get young people "swinging from the trees"; it is to help them cling to the Vine *(cf. John 15)*.

Any number of factors can short-circuit this important work. But, ultimately, the key to preventing a nasty fall is to restore balance to the way we do youth ministry. What follows are some of the most common errors of imbalance in traditional, Protestant, North American youth ministries. Admittedly, they are anecdotal and personal in nature. As such, they are not so much conclusive as they are suggestive. But perhaps these observations will at least provoke questions and further discussion.

Imbalance #1: Too Much Arrival, Not Enough Survival

The Christian life is a marathon. It is not about speed; it is about distance. It is not about how fast our young people grow; it is about how far our young people grow.[7] If we want to nurture in our students a faith that does not fail, we need to focus on strategies that encourage survival and not just arrival. There is nowhere in Scripture where we are called to make Christians. Only God can make Christians. Our mandate as youth workers is to make disciples *(cf. Matthew 28:19; 2 Timothy 2:2)*. That is not to say that outreach is unimportant. Obviously, the church is called to give witness to Jesus *(Acts 1:8)*. Those who pit discipleship against evangelism do not understand that evangelism is the first stage in the process of discipleship. No one has ever been discipled who was not first evangelized.

Youth ministry has a growing number of what might be described as "discipleship snobs"—youth workers who talk about evangelism and outreach as if it were a lower life-form of youth ministry. "I don't have time to mess around with kids who aren't interested in doing something radical for Jesus! I didn't get into the ministry so I could do fun and games."

Standing on the beach one day, Jesus looked squarely into Peter's eyes and said, "From now on you will be catching people" *(Luke 5:10)*. As a fisherman, Peter knew it takes two things to catch fish: a net and patience. Whether we like it or not, fishing for people will always involve both. Fish don't just report to the boat.

On the other hand, no person who fishes continues to catch fish without giving some thought to how he or she will preserve them and keep them fresh. Otherwise, at the end of the day, all the person has to show for his or her labor is a big boat filled with smelly, dead fish. Big catch. Big deal.

The problem is that catching fish is more exhilarating than scaling them, cleaning them, and preserving them. Evangelism generates greater excitement and bigger numbers than discipleship and nurture.

There is always more excitement in the arrival than there is in survival. There are hugs and kisses and animated conversations when the guests first arrive. Who wouldn't want to focus their ministry on that end of the equation? After a few days of sharing the bathroom and cleaning up someone else's mess, we begin the mundane work of life in shared community. That is not quite as exhilarating.

So much of our youth ministry effort is focused on helping young people to "become Christians" that we have lost sight of our central God-given mandate. One study of church young people indicates that we are doing a better job of getting them to show up than we are at helping them to grow up.

- Six out of ten say there is no such thing as absolute truth.
- Nine out of ten say that right and wrong depend on the individual and the situation—that is, they espouse moral relativism.
- One out of four deny the notion that acting in disobedience to God's laws brings about negative consequences.
- One-half believe the main purpose of life is enjoyment and personal fulfillment.
- One out of three say that as long as something works, you can be sure that it is morally or ethically right.
- About half of the Christian teens in American maintain that people can earn their way into heaven through good works and exemplary behavior.[8]

Our task in youth ministry is not just helping young people to become Christians; it is helping young people to be the Christians they have become. There is nothing wrong with cookouts, ski trips, movie nights, and bowling parties that draw a big crowd. But when all is said and done, we dare not focus so much on getting kids to arrive that we neglect the hard, less glamorous work of helping them to survive.

Imbalance #2: Too Often Childish, Not Enough Childlike

It's too bad that real life is not a flannel graph. It would be so much easier if we could reduce all the hassles, temptations, and questions of life to a few cutout felt figures. But real life doesn't always match the Sunday school simplicity of four or five figures clinging to a flannel background. Perhaps it is this oversimplification[9] that has bred a generation of teenage "Tarzan Christians" who come away from spiritual highs beating their chests and swinging through the treetops but too often end up lost, demoralized, and defeated down on the jungle floor.

Surely at the heart of this oversimplification is the tendency of the church in general, and youth ministry in particular, to nurture in our students what pastoral theologian and counselor David Seamands describes as a "childish faith."[10]

It's a jungle out there. We chop a path for our children around some of these questions during their younger years, and rightly so. But, there comes a point at which the questions and dangers of the adolescent jungle are too many and too thick. All of a sudden our teenagers discover that the flannel graph didn't tell the whole story. Doubt is a predictable part of adolescence. Some of our students make it through this thick undergrowth of questions with their faith intact and strengthened. Some of our students end up losing the trail.

The apostle Paul alludes to just this part of the adolescent safari when he writes, "When I was a child, I spoke like a child, I thought like a child, I reasoned like a child; when I became an adult, I put an end to childish ways" *(1 Corinthians 13:11)*. What Paul seems to be saying is that spiritual maturity involves giving up a childish faith that believes in easy answers, and holding tight to a childlike faith that trusts the Father even when there doesn't seem to be any answer. Putting away childish reasoning means nothing less and nothing more than helping students to forge a path through the jungle marked, not by simple, easy half-truths, but by durable, biblical hard truths. That doesn't mean that we are in any sense to attempt to explain away the wonder and mystery of God. What it does mean is that we help the students in our youth group come to grips with the fact that life doesn't always look like the flannel graph.

Notice in the chart the differences between "childish faith" and childlike faith.

In their book, *The Godbearing Life: The Art of Soul-Tending for Youth Ministry,* Dean and Foster observe,

> Despite our substantial experience involving young people in practices of teaching and nurture, evidence suggests that we have not effectively used these practices to help young people mature in their faith. About two youth in five participate in Christian education programs, and 45 percent of American adolescents say religion is less important to them than to their parents. Confirmation, the rite of passage adopted by many mainline traditions as an entry into the adult Christian community, has more often been treated as graduation out of it. In a study of five hundred people confirmed in the Presbyterian Church as teenagers, nearly half (48 percent) were unchurched by the time they reached their mid-thirties.[11]

Perhaps if we were to nurture in our young people something more than a childish faith, they would find it more relevant when they are no longer children. Tarzan Christianity happens when we root students in

Childish Faith	Childlike Faith
Good Christians don't have pain and disappointments.	God uses our pain and disappointment to make us better Christians.
God helps those who help themselves.	God can only begin to help those who admit their own helplessness.
God wants to make us happy.	God wants to make us holy.
God always answers prayer.	Sometimes God answers with "No" or "Wait."
Faith will help us to always understand what God is doing.	Faith will help us to stand under God's sovereignty even when we don't have a clue what God is doing.
The closer we get to God, the more perfect we become.	The closer we get to God, the more we become aware of our own sinfulness.
Mature Christians don't wrestle with the tough questions of doubt and struggle.	Mature Christians can wrestle honestly with tough questions because we trust that God has the answers.
Good Christians are always strong.	Our strength is in admitting our weakness.

a nice, clean, childish flannel graph faith instead of the childlike trusting faith to which the Scripture calls us *(Matthew 19:13-14)*.

Could an honest approach to these tough questions cause some discomfort for our students? To be sure. But as one writer describes it, growing young faith is like throwing rocks in a pond. When the rocks hit the pond, the expanding ripples move outward to shore from the place where the stone splashed in. "Teaching for faith...breaks the water's surface, creating a disturbance that calls forth new rings of faith. We can think [of these] disturbances in our faith life as growing pains, times of stretching beyond our present self toward a deeper and more profound relationship with God."[12]

Imbalance #3: Too Much Feel Good, Not Enough Think Well

Neil Postman opens his excellent book *Amusing Ourselves to Death* with a profound and arresting quote. In drawing a distinction between two popular notions about what the future might be, he comments,

> What Orwell feared were those who would ban books. What Huxley feared was that there would be no reason to ban a book, for there would be no one who wanted to read one. Orwell feared those who would deprive us of information. Huxley feared those who would give us so much that we would be reduced to passivity and egoism. Orwell feared that the truth would be concealed from us. Huxley feared the truth drowned in a sea of irrelevance. Orwell feared we would become a captive culture. Huxley feared we would become a trivial culture, preoccupied with some equivalent of the feelies, the orgy porgy, and the centrifugal bumblepuppy. As Huxley remarked in *Brave New World Revisited,* the civil libertarians and rationalists who are ever on the alert to oppose tyranny "failed to take into account man's almost infinite appetite for distractions." In *1984,* Huxley added, people are controlled by inflicting pain. In *Brave New World,* they are controlled by inflicting pleasure. In short, Orwell feared that what we hate will ruin us. Huxley feared that what we love will ruin us. This book is about the possibility that Huxley, not Orwell, was right.[13]

Had Postman been aware of the current climate in youth ministry, he would have found his alarm only confirmed. The church in general, and youth ministry in particular, has demonstrated more of an appetite for goosebumps than for God's truth, more interest in how our young people feel than how they think, more enchantment with the latest CD than with the latest book. In short, we have become all heart and no head.

A personal experience comes to mind: Not long ago a youth leader approached me just prior to the last session of a weeklong camp. It had been a wonderful camp, and she had thought of the perfect way to finish out the week.

"I brought this CD with the song 'Thank you, Lord.' Why don't we play it for the kids in this last session?"

Being a little unclear why she was suggesting this to me since I had zero authority to make any decisions, I encouraged her to talk to the folks in charge of the event.

And that's when she said, "Okay, I'll do that. But I think it would really be great. Every time I've played it at other camps, everybody has cried."

It was a totally sincere comment from a bighearted leader who loved her students and wanted to maximize their experience at that week of camp. But the premise that lay behind it was what troubled me: If we can find a way to get all the kids crying, it must be a good programming idea. In other words, one of her criteria for evaluating a youth ministry idea was very simple: Does it make kids cry? Does it move them emotionally? If it does, it must be worthy.

Perhaps in this technological age we have so come to desire the human touch that we have settled upon the notion that any experience is validated by its emotional impact—by its ability to move us emotionally. It is understandable that youth workers would think this way. Their constituents—the young people—have been taught to evaluate every experience by one of two criteria: it was either "good" or "boring."

Perhaps this is also the overflow of educational theorists who seem to be embarrassed by the transfer of information, who have encouraged us to move away from teaching children facts and have identified the central task of the classroom as making all the students feel good about themselves.[14] As James Ferguson put it, speaking as the principal of

Heritage High School in Littleton, Colorado, "It is more important for me to have students know how to read a map than for them to have any one bit of information about that map. Rather than knowing where Nepal is, it's more important that they know how to find Nepal." (In an earlier quote, Ferguson had actually opined that students needn't be able to find Florida. He later made the change to Nepal, presumably because Nepal seems so much more remote and therefore manifestly not as important.)

The thrust of Ferguson's comment seems quite clear: It is not important for students to learn specific facts.

In his book *Dumbing Down Our Kids: Why American Children Feel Good about Themselves but Can't Read, Write or Add,* author Charles Sykes goes on to report of Ferguson:

> He specifically denied that high school students needed to be able to define either the Holocaust or World War II. When pressed, the educational leader would not even agree that a high school graduate should know something about the Great Depression. In one interview he implied that there was something unfair about singling out some historical landmarks as more important than others, a selection that was arbitrary, judgmental, and impertinent....In other words, students can be taught something called "map reading skills" or "geographical thinking."[15]

It's an interesting analogy, because it is reminiscent of C. S Lewis's comment about a conversation he once had with an old crusty R.A.F. officer who complained that he had little need for Lewis's discussions of theology and doctrine, for he had felt God's presence: out alone in the desert at night, he had sensed this mysterious, tremendous presence.

> Now in a sense I quite agreed with that man. I think he had probably had a real experience of God in the desert. And when he turned from that experience to the Christian creeds, I think he really was turning from something real to something less real. In the same way, if a man has once looked at the Atlantic from the beach, and then goes and looks at a map of the Atlantic, he also will be turning from something real to something less real: turning from real

waves to a bit of colored paper. But here comes the point. The map is admittedly only colored paper, but there are two things you have to remember about it. In the first place, it is based on what hundreds and thousands of people have found by sailing the real Atlantic. In that way it has behind it masses of experience just as real as the one you could have from the beach; only, while yours would be a single isolated glimpse, the map fits all those different experiences together. In the second place, if you want to go anywhere, the map is absolutely necessary. As long as you are content with walks on the beach, your own glimpses are far more fun than looking at a map. But the map is going to be more use than walks on the beach if you want to get to America.[16]

In short, our affection for creating emotional experiences and giving adolescents "warm fuzzies," coupled with our reluctance to teach biblical theology, is sending students to sea without any map. Our young people have become incapable of theological thinking because they do not have any theology to think about. Their faith is all heart (what they've felt of that "mysterious, tremendous presence") and not much head. And, as Paul warns us, it is this combination that leaves us as "children, tossed to and fro and blown about by every wind of doctrine" *(Ephesians 4:14).*

Imbalance #4: Too Much How, Not Enough Why

Perhaps most troubling about the current state of youth ministry in North America is its infatuation with technique. Youth workers are far more concerned about how than about what or why—technique is what captures the imagination, not what we should be doing or why we are doing it.[17] Indeed, in a conversation with the director of product development for one of the country's largest publishers of youth ministry resources, when asked if it might be advisable that there be some print given to deeper issues of vision and theology, he replied with apparent surprise, "Ought we to be talking to folks about vision?"

Ought we indeed? Why can't we just be satisfied with training youth workers in general how to do nothing in particular? What's wrong with doing nothing, but doing it creatively and effectively?

What's wrong is that our culture is obsessed with technique. But *how* without *why* is vapid and bankrupt. This is the same approach that assumes more books about how to have sex will breed deeper intimacy and greater sexual satisfaction. Any talk about love or commitment is tedious and tangential. Unfortunately, it is precisely this sort of approach that has given us a culture in which marriages disintegrate with alarming frequency and sexual dissatisfaction seems to be far more prominent.

To be sure, youth ministry training in North America is market-driven, and that is fair and understandable. But to what extent does the marketplace take over our calling as youth workers to consider deeper issues? Should educators be trained how to teach without regard for the content they are teaching? Is the real key for medical training to make sure that aspiring doctors be taught bedside manners and injection techniques? Or should even greater attention be given to the question of what "healthy" looks like? Most of us would prefer a physician who has had training in both.

This is why Eugene Peterson distinguishes between "a job" and "a profession or craft."[18] He defines a job as what we do to complete an assignment. It is focused on execution. We learn what is expected by those to whom we are responsible, and we do it. A profession, on the other hand, brings with it an obligation beyond pleasing somebody; "we are pursuing or shaping the very nature of reality, convinced that when we carry out our commitments we actually benefit people at a far deeper level than if we simply did what they asked of us."[19] Here the emphasis turns to why and what. "For physicians it is health (not merely making people feel good); with lawyers, justice (not helping people get their own way); with professors, learning (not merely cramming cranial cavities with information on tap for examinations). And with pastors it is God (not relieving anxiety, or giving comfort, or running a religious establishment)."[20] Nor is it simply effective organization of a youth ministry that starts and ends on time with adequate food provided.

Please understand that there is nothing wrong with doing a job, and youth ministry in particular is a very tough job. "How-to" books are especially helpful to laypeople who are already time-stressed and undertrained. Even professional long-term youth workers can appreciate the value of having an arsenal of resources that speak to the "how-to" issues. In that sense, it is worthy and appropriate to develop, publish, and provide training in the area of technique.[21]

But if we go no deeper and no further, we have traded off our calling and our profession to be little more than peddlers. Unfortunately, if that is our approach, we begin to dumb down the prescription to fit the patient's diagnosis.[22] The patient wants a quick fix to ease the pain of the Sunday night meeting. The wise doctor will want to think with the patient about what in the meeting is causing the pain and, more importantly, what does a healthy ministry look like? We need youth ministry books, training, and resources that ask not just how but what and why.

It's a Jungle out There

These observations are incomplete and thus deserve further attention and thought. And unless we address some of these concerns, we will continue to see Tarzan Christians emerge from our youth programs, and many of them get lost in the jungle.

The burden of this chapter is that most of these questions are never raised—in part, at least, because they require that we stop the machinery and check for the proverbial "wrench in the works." No one wants to do that.

Which is probably why the church, and youth ministry especially, has over the last fifteen years so needed the voice of Tony Campolo. He may not be the most beloved doctor in town, but he never shrinks from making the tough diagnosis. Hopefully, the words of this chapter from one of Campolo's friends and admirers will be received in that spirit. "Faithful are the wounds of a friend."

5/
Why Would Anybody Ever Want to Be an Evangelical?

Ronald J. Sider

This chapter was originally presented to a secular audience at Colorado College, Colorado, on January 22, 1994, at a college-wide conference on spirituality. I was the "token evangelical." Perhaps this essay designed for such a setting is an appropriate piece to honor a man who has regularly been an evangelist/apologist to secular contemporaries.

AREN'T EVANGELICALS THE FOLKS who bring us TV evangelists with their sex scandals? Aren't evangelicals right-wing fanatics who fight all sensible gun control? Aren't evangelicals antifeminist reactionaries who want their women in the kitchen, submissive, barefoot, and pregnant? Don't they want to take away the civil rights of gay Americans? And aren't they intellectual obscurantists who reject modern science? Don't they destroy the environment because they think the world is going to end very soon, so we might as well use all we can before God blows it to bits?

The public image of evangelicals is not very good. At worst, evangelicals are seen by many Americans as dangerous threats to freedom, justice, and the environment. At best, they are seen as naïve, reactionary folk who want to return to the Middle Ages. Or they may be seen as silly, superstitious legalists.

The popular stereotype of evangelicals, however, is far too simplistic. Some evangelicals do fit the stereotype, but I'm also an evangelical and I don't fit that image. I'm a feminist. I defend civil rights for gay Americans. I support vigorous gun control legislation. I'm the leader of a Christian environmental organization. I have worked hard for justice for the poor and for nuclear disarmament. In fact, I debated Religious Right leader Jerry Falwell on the nuclear freeze issue in the early '80s. I was in favor of a nuclear freeze, while Jerry opposed it!

The widespread stereotype that all evangelicals are right-wing fanatics is simply wrong. Well, then, who are the evangelicals?

First of all, they are a big group. A 1992 Gallup Poll estimated that evangelicals make up 38 percent of the American population. A very careful study by four political scientists in 1992 discovered that there are almost exactly as many Protestant evangelicals in the United States as Catholics: each are about 23 percent of the total population. That translates into 43 million voters.

What do these people believe? Their core beliefs are the following:
1. The historic Christian affirmations about Jesus of Nazareth are true. Jesus is true God as well a true man, the only Savior who died for our sins and rose again from the dead.
2. The Old Testament and New Testament are a special, authoritative revelation from God and, for Protestant evangelicals, the final source for what we should believe and how we should act.
3. Telling others about Jesus Christ and inviting others to follow him are a central part of Christian faith.

Beyond some core beliefs that all evangelicals share, there is much diversity in church life and political viewpoint. Let me illustrate this in terms of political views using the 1992 study by the political scientists I mentioned earlier.

Most, although not all, evangelicals are prolife and oppose abortion. Virtually all evangelicals believe homosexual practice is contrary to God's will. But the political scientists found that a majority of evangelicals also favor a number of political stands that are usually identified as progressive or liberal rather than conservative. A majority of evangelicals favor national health insurance, good government programs to reduce poverty, and environmental initiatives.

Evangelicals have had bad press. The stereotypes don't fit many of us. I invite you to set aside those defective images, if only for the present, and explore with me what evangelicals believe and do and why they think and do that.

Of necessity, I must sketch a broad outline. I'm aware that every sentence needs a book (or ten) to substantiate the claims being made.

Evangelicals think that many modern thinkers have committed intellectual suicide. Modern people claim that humans, indeed all living things, are merely the product of a blind materialistic process governed by chance. Modern science, they claim, proves that. That is the viewpoint that still dominates the universities, the media, and the intelligentsia generally. I have recently been involved in a major project on the environment with Carl Sagan and others. Carl Sagan, who died very recently of cancer, illustrated this huge mistake of modern thinkers. At the beginning of Cosmos (the book and the TV series), Sagan says nature is all that is, was, and ever shall be.

Notice what follows if they are right. If everything results from matter and chance, then truth and ethics do not exist. People are simply sophisticated materialistic machines. Ethical values are totally subjective, merely an expression of our individual feelings. As the famous secular philosopher and mathematician Bertrand Russell said, ethical beliefs are totally relative.

In fact, Russell said that those who have the best poison gas will determine the ethics of the future. Ethics is what the powerful say is right. According to Marxist ethics, whatever served the interest of the party was true and good. Human life is not sacred and can be destroyed at society's convenience. If this supposedly "scientific" view is correct, then truth and ethics are illusions. Persons are machines. Truth, justice, freedom, responsibility, and liberty disappear. Society self-destructs.

Christians have a radically *different* view of the world.[1] We believe that all life is the creation of a loving personal God, although some believe God may have used a complex evolutionary process to do that. Human beings are free responsible persons whose deepest joy and ultimate obligation is to live in right relationship with their loving Creator. Created in God's image, every human being has ultimate value. Ethical truths are an expression of the very nature of God, not a relativistic product of a blind materialistic process.

Christians have believed these things for centuries. How did the modern secular view arise? It arose in the eighteenth century when more and more thinkers mistakenly concluded that one could not believe both in modern science and miracles at the same time. Consequently, modern thinkers rejected the view held by Christians for 1,800 years that Jesus is true God and that he rose from the dead. They abandoned the belief that persons are created in the image of God and called to respond to God and live forever in God's presence. Instead, they saw people as complex machines produced by a blind, materialistic process and destined to decay and disappear like the grass, the trees, and the worms.

It is very important to understand this basic mistake in modern thought. It is sheer confusion to suppose that more and more scientific information makes belief in God the Creator or belief in miracles more and more intellectually irresponsible. Science simply tells us with greater and greater precision what nature regularly does. In principle, no amount of scientific information could ever tell us whether there might or might not be a God who exists outside of nature. Now if an all-powerful God happened to exist outside nature, that God could intervene in nature anytime God chose. Does such a being exist?

One way to look for an answer to that question is to ask whether there is any evidence that points to the existence of such a God. I was trained at Yale as a historian. As a historian I think the historical evidence we have about Jesus of Nazareth points in that direction.

Over the centuries, Christians have claimed two very unusual things about Jesus: (1) in addition to being a great ethical teacher, he was also God in the flesh; (2) after being crucified, he returned to life after three days.

If modern thinkers are right, if blind materialistic process is all there is, then resurrection from the dead is impossible. But if God exists, then resurrection from the dead would be possible anytime God chose to do that. If there was good historical evidence to show that Jesus was truly alive on the third day, that would also strongly suggest that God exists. Interestingly, Anthony Flew said something similar a few years ago. Flew, as you know, is one of the great modern philosophers. He is also a prominent secular agnostic. But listen to what Flew says about Jesus' resurrection: "We are agreed that the question of whether Jesus did rise from the dead is of supreme theoretical and practical importance. For the knowable fact that he did, if indeed it is a knowable fact, is the best if not the only reason for accepting that Jesus is the God of Abraham, Isaac and Israel."[2]

Well, what evidence is there?

Before we ask about the historical evidence for Jesus' resurrection, however, I want to sketch two other important historical facts about Jesus of Nazareth. First, Jesus was a radical guy. He challenged the status quo of his time in all kinds of ways.

Rich and Poor

Jesus shocked the rich with his words about sharing. He told the rich young man who came inquiring about eternal life (and probably about membership in Jesus' new circle as well) that he would have to sell his vast holdings and give all his wealth to the poor. Jesus urged the rich to make loans to the poor even if there was no reasonable hope of repayment *(Luke 6:34-35)*. Those who do not feed the hungry and clothe the naked, he said, will go to hell *(Matthew 25:31-46)*.

The Marginalized

Jesus' special concern for the poor extended to all the marginalized, weak, and socially ostracized. In sharp contrast to his contemporaries, Jesus demonstrated a special interest in the disabled, children, drunkards, prostitutes, and lepers *(cf. Luke 7:32-50; 19:1-10)*. In Jesus' day lepers experienced terrible ostracism *(Luke 17:12)*, living alone in awful poverty, shouting "unclean, unclean" lest anyone accidentally touch them. Jesus gently touched the lepers and miraculously healed them *(Mark 1:41)*.

From the Dead Sea Scrolls we learn that the Essenes, a Jewish religious group of Jesus' day, actually *excluded* the disabled from the religious community: "No one who is afflicted with any human impurity may come into the assembly of God....Anyone who is...maimed in hand or foot, lame or blind or deaf or dumb or with a visible mark in his flesh.…These may not enter or take their place in the midst of the community."[3] Jesus, by contrast, commands the members of his new messianic community to invite *precisely* these people: "When you give a banquet, invite the poor, the crippled, the lame, and the blind" *(Luke 14:13).*

Women

Jesus' attitude toward women reflects the same sweeping challenge to the status quo. In Jesus' day it was a scandal for a man to appear in public with a woman. A woman's word was considered useless in court. It was better to burn a copy of the Torah (the first five books of the Hebrew Bible) than to allow a woman to touch it. Indeed, according to one first-century statement, "If any man teach his daughter Torah, it is as though he taught her lechery." Women were excluded from most parts of the temple. Nor did they count in calculating the quorum needed for a meeting in the synagogue. First-century Jewish men regularly thanked God that they were not Gentiles, slaves, or women.

Jesus and his new community rejected centuries of male prejudice and treated women as equals. Jesus appeared with women in public *(John 4:27)* and taught them theology *(Luke 10:38-42).* He allowed a woman who everyone knew was a sinner to wash his feet with her tears, wipe them with her long hair, and kiss and perfume them—all in public *(Luke 7:36-50).* Absolutely scandalous! When Mary abandoned her traditional role of cooking food to listen to Jesus' theology lesson, Martha objected. But Jesus defended Mary *(Luke 10:38-42).*

Jesus also challenged men in another way. Jesus rejected Moses' teaching on divorce, which allowed a man (but not a woman) to dismiss his spouse if she did not find favor in his eyes *(Deuteronomy 24:12).* Jesus called both husband and wife to live together in lifelong covenant *(Mark 10:1-12).*

It was surely no accident that Jesus granted the first resurrection appearance to women!

Political Leadership

Jesus must have infuriated Herod. When someone warned him that Herod wanted to kill him, Jesus shot back his response: "Go and tell that fox…"*(Luke 13:32).* In Jesus' day, that word meant about the same thing as the slang use of the word skunk does today. Jesus taught and lived a radical ethic that deeply challenged the status quo. That alone probably would have been enough to get him put away.

But Jesus did another thing. He made outrageous claims about himself. He claimed divine authority to forgive sins. The religious leaders rightly said only God could do that. Jesus placed his own authority above that of Moses. And at his trial he acknowledged that he was the Son of God.

So Jesus got killed—for two reasons! First, because he was a dangerous social radical. Second, because they said he was a blasphemer who claimed to be the only Son of God.

So he was crucified. And that would seem to have put an end to Jesus. Except for one thing. Soon after his death, there were reports that he was alive again.

Now, I have been trained as an historian. I did my doctoral work at Yale in history. I'm as skeptical as you are about silly claims with no evidence. Is there any solid evidence that this carpenter from Nazareth was really alive on the third day?

I have examined the historical evidence carefully. Thousands of articles and hundreds of books have been written on the topic. Here I can only summarize my research in four quick points: (1) the change in the discouraged disciples; (2) the empty tomb; (3) the fact that the first witnesses were women; and (4) the very early evidence in 1 Corinthians 15.

A short time after the crucifixion, the disciples announced to a Jerusalem crowd that Jesus had been raised from the dead. Within a few years, these same disciples proceeded to crisscross the eastern part of the Roman Empire, braving intense persecution and eventually experiencing martyrdom. Yet it was these very people who had scattered at Jesus' arrest and fled home in despair.

What gave rise to the "resurrection faith" and the disciples' willingness to risk their lives to spread it? Professor Reginald H. Fuller, formerly of New York's Union Theological Seminary, has underlined the fact that this total transformation demands explanation: "Even the most skeptical historian has to postulate an X, as M. Dibelius called it, to account for the complete change in the behavior of the disciples, who at Jesus' arrest had fled and scattered to their own homes, but who in a few weeks were boldly preaching their message to the very people who had sought to crush the movement launched by Jesus."[4]

Professor Pinchas Lapide, a prominent European Jewish scholar, makes the same point in a recent book, *The Resurrection of Jesus.* Lapide is not a Christian, but he does believe Jesus was alive on the third day.

> I am completely convinced that the twelve from Galilee, who were all farmers, shepherds and fishermen—there was not a single theology professor to be found among them— were totally unimpressed by scholarly theologumena, as Karl Rahner and Rudolf Bultmann write them. If they, through such a concrete historical event as the crucifixion, were so totally in despair and crushed, as all four evangelists report to us, then no less concrete a historical event was needed in order to bring them out of the deep valley of their despair and within a short time transform them into a community of salvation rejoicing to the high heavens.[5]

Lapide also writes,

> When this scared, frightened band of the apostles which was just about to throw away everything in order to flee in despair to Galilee; when these peasants, shepherds and fishermen who betrayed and denied their master and then failed him miserably, suddenly could be changed overnight into a confident mission society convinced of salvation and able to work with much more success after Easter than before Easter, then no vision or hallucination is sufficient to explain such a revolutionary transformation.[6]

The explanation of the people closest to the events was that Jesus of Nazareth arose from the tomb and appeared to them over a period of a number of days.

If one rejects the New Testament explanation of the resurrection faith and the transformation it caused in extremely discouraged people, then one is left with the very difficult task of proposing other grounds adequate to explain it. The late Professor Robert Grant of the University of Chicago has said: "The origin of Christianity is almost incomprehensible unless such an event took place."[7]

Second, and very important, is the question of the empty tomb. A short time after the crucifixion, Peter claimed that Jesus arose from the dead, and note that he made the claim in Jerusalem. It is exceedingly significant that the controversy over the resurrection, and the rise of the first church, took place precisely in Jerusalem where anybody could have gone to visit the place of burial. It was in Jerusalem that hundreds became Christians within months of Jesus' death. Obviously it was in the interests of the religious leaders to produce the body of Jesus or give clear evidence of its proper disposal. But the earliest counterargument against the claim that Jesus was alive was the suggestion that the disciples had stolen the body. This was an acknowledgment that they could not produce the body.

A number of attempts have been made to explain the empty tomb. The old one of the theft is no longer accepted. It has been suggested that Joseph of Arimathea, or the Romans, or the Jewish leaders removed the body before the women arrived; but if so, the Jewish leaders would surely have conducted guided tours to the real burial place as soon as the silly disciples claimed Jesus had arisen.

In his discussion of Jesus' resurrection, Professor Wolfhart Pannenberg quotes Paul Althaus to underline this point:

Paul Althaus has rightly seen this point: "In Jerusalem, the place of Jesus' execution and grave, it was proclaimed not long after his death that he had been raised. The situation demands that within the circle of the first community one had a reliable testimony for the fact that the grave had been found empty." The resurrection kerygma "could not have been maintained in Jerusalem for a single day, for a single hour, if the emptiness of the tomb had not been established as a fact for all concerned."[8]

Since, then, the Christians and those who disagreed with them both agreed that the tomb was empty, it seems very likely that the empty tomb is a historical fact.

Third, the fact that women were the first people to visit the tomb and allegedly see the risen Jesus speaks in favor of the authenticity of the accounts. Professor C. F. D. Moule of Cambridge has pointed out that women were notoriously invalid witnesses according to Jewish principles of evidence.[9] If, then, the early Christians had fabricated the accounts of the first visit to the tomb and the first meeting with the risen

Jesus, they certainly would have claimed that men were the first witnesses. The best explanation for the priority of the women is that it actually happened that way.

Finally, we must look at the oldest evidence for the resurrection. In his first letter to the Corinthian church (the date is about A.D. 50-55), Paul wrote,

> I handed on to you as of first importance what I in turn had received: that Christ died for our sins in accordance with the scriptures, and that he was buried, and that he was raised on the third day in accordance with the scriptures, and that he appeared to Cephas, then to the twelve. Then he appeared to more than five hundred brothers and sisters at one time, most of whom are still alive, though some have died. Then he appeared to James, then to all the apostles. Last of all, as to one untimely born, he appeared also to me.
> *(1 Corinthians 15:3-8)*

Paul implies that, if his readers do not believe him, they can check, for many of the eyewitnesses are still around. In fact, the eyewitnesses on both sides saw the rapid spread of Christianity from Jerusalem to Rome.

The most important aspect of this passage, however, is its early date. Many scholars have pointed out that the words used here ("handed on" and "received") are technical terms used to refer to the careful handing down of oral tradition.[10] Paul apparently taught this to all the churches. Furthermore, Paul says he received it presumably soon after he became a Christian about A.D. 35, just a few years after Jesus' death. That means that this witness to Jesus' resurrection received a fixed form very soon after the actual events (quite possibly before Paul's first postconversion visit to Jerusalem about A.D. 36 *[Galatians 1:18-19]*).

As a historian, I find the evidence surprisingly strong. The most unbiased historical conclusion is that Jesus was probably alive on the third day.

How did that happen? Obviously, you and I cannot do that sort of thing even with all our modern technology. The first Christians said God raised Jesus from the dead. That seems to me to be the most reasonable explanation. The resurrection suggests that the Christian view of the world, not the modern secular one, is true.

The resurrection is central both to what Christians think and to what they do at all kinds of points. Briefly, I mention three implications or results of Jesus' resurrection.

First, the resurrection radically transformed what Jesus' followers thought about Jesus himself. Before the resurrection, Jesus' followers called him "Master," "Rabbi," "Teacher." Afterward, they called him "Messiah," "Son of God," "Lord." This word *lord* (Greek *kurios*) is very important. The word *kurios* was used in the Greek translation of the old Testament to translate the word *Jahweh*—the name for the one God at the center of Jewish monotheism. This is the word that became one of the most frequently used titles for the man from Nazareth. In Philippians 2, Paul applied to Jesus the words from Isaiah 45:23, which the monotheistic prophet had used for Jahweh. After mocking the idols, Jahweh insisted in Isaiah 45:23 that he alone was God: "To me every knee shall bow, every tongue shall swear" *(Isaiah 45:23)*. The rabbinically trained Paul—one of the most uncompromising monotheists in his day—took those words from the mouth of Jahweh and applied them to Jesus, declaring that "at the name of Jesus every knee should bend, in heaven and on earth and under the earth, and every tongue should confess that Jesus Christ is Lord" *(Philippians 2:10-11)*. The carpenter is *kurios*—God.

It is here that modern people take offense. Almost everyone is happy to acknowledge Jesus as the greatest prophet of all time, the most profound ethical teacher of human history. But Christians persist in pointing out that he was true God as well as true man. That offends. Christians remember his words "I am the way, and the truth, and the life. No one comes to the Father except through me" *(John 14:6)*. That offends.

If Jesus was God in the flesh, however, then I cannot pick and choose among Jesus' teachings, accepting the things I like and rejecting those that don't feel good. Instead, I must joyfully accept him as Lord of all of my life—my politics, my economics, and my sexual life.

But Jesus taught some pretty costly things about sharing with the poor, loving my enemies, and keeping my marriage covenant for life. And I often find it hard to do what he said.

It's just at this point that a second implication of Jesus' resurrection is so important. The New Testament says that when people believe in Jesus Christ, then the same divine power that raised Jesus from the dead now works in believers to empower them to live the way Jesus did.

Just as Christ died and was raised, so by faith we can die to the old life of selfishness and rise to a new life in Christ. "We have been buried with him by baptism into death, so that, just as Christ was raised from the dead by the glory of the Father, so we too might walk in newness of life" *(Romans 6:4)*. Or as Paul puts it in Galatians, the risen Lord now lives in those who believe in Him: "It is no longer I who live, but it is Christ who lives in me" *(Galatians 2:20)*. "Christ in us" will mean living for Christ's sake a life for others. It may mean losing a job because we will not participate in the manufacture of nuclear weapons. It may mean rejecting or abandoning an attractive position in Toronto or Vancouver in order to work with the poor in the Third World. It may mean deciding to live in the scarred inner city rather than in the pleasant suburbs. It will certainly mean risking the disapproval of our friends, colleagues, and parishioners by clearly and persistently announcing the biblical word that God is on the side of the poor and that he calls us to be peacemakers. Because Christ lives in us, we have the spiritual energy to choose the difficult. We will be able to exhibit the same kind of love Christ revealed in dying for us precisely because the God who raised our Lord Jesus now raises us to a new life for others.

Finally, the Christian view of death is my third illustration of how Jesus' resurrection radically shapes what Christians think.

Over the ages, death has seemed to pose a terrifying threat. Modern secular people, of course, pretend otherwise. Bertrand Russell assures us that there is no need to tremble at the idea that death ends personal existence forever. We die, rot, and that's it. Most people merely buy life insurance and try not to think about it. But what ultimate meaning does personal existence possess if it exists for three score years or, perhaps by reason of modern medicine, four score years, and then passes into sheer nothingness?

The Marxist philosopher Ernst Bloch thinks that the relative neglect of the problem of death in modern secular thought is due to the unconscious influence of inherited Christian views.

Death (we do not know for how long) can only be sup-
pressed so well because new life was once hidden behind it;
that is, it was dreamed about and believed to be there....The
paltry confession to nothing *(Nichts)* would hardly be suffi-
cient to keep the head high and to work as if there were no
end. Rather clear signs indicate that earlier and richer forms
of wishful dreams [?] continue and give support in the sub-
conscious. Through what remains from these ideals, the so-
called modern man does not feel the chasm that unceasing-
ly surrounds him and that certainly will engulf him at last.
Through these remnants he saves, quite unawares, his sense
of self-identity. Through them the impression arises that
man is not perishing....Thus in its ability to suppress the
anxiety of all earlier times, apparently this quite shallow
courage [of modern secular] people feasts on a borrowed
credit card. It lives from earlier hopes and the support that
they once had provided.[11]

Christians appreciate Bloch's expose of secular shallowness in the
face of the ultimate reality of death. But we insist that the ancient hope
for life after death is not wishful dreaming but assured reality.
Christians believe that death is not a terrifying passage into nothingness but rather a transition into a glorious eternity in the presence of
the Risen Lord Jesus. Why do Christians believe that? Because one person, Jesus of Nazareth, has already experienced death in all its fullness
and returned from the dead to live forever. Christians believe that
death is not a terrifying threat because the tomb was empty, because
the one with whom the disciples had lived appeared to them and
assured them that he is alive forevermore. We await the risen Lord
Jesus, and therefore can declare with Paul: "'Death has been swal-
lowed up in victory.' 'Where, O death, is your victory? Where, O
death, is your sting?'...Thanks be to God, who gives us the victory
through our Lord Jesus Christ" *(1 Corinthians 15:54-57).*

With this view of death, the Christian can act courageously today.
Life at any cost is not our motto; death for the King's cause is not disastrous. Paul says: "If we live, we live to the Lord, and if we die, we
die to the Lord....For to this end Christ died and lived again, so that

he might be Lord of both the dead and the living" *(Romans 14:8-9).* Because Christ is Lord of the living and the dead, we dare to face racists and militarists for the sake of our sisters and brothers; we dare to go as missionaries into dangerous situations; we dare to leave comfortable classrooms and secure homes to try to apply Jesus' call to peace and justice in the halls of government; we dare to join the poor in the swirling abyss of oppressive situations around the world. Jesus' resurrection has transformed what Christians think and what Christians seek to do.

But closing, I want to show how the kind of evangelical Christianity I am describing works out concretely in the tough issues of our time— our ravaged environment, our violence-torn inner cities, and our devastated families. And I'm going to make a strong claim that I'm sure some will want to challenge. I'm going to argue that biblical Christianity offers a better solution to these and other problems than the alternatives people are trying.

First a word on methodology. Whenever I seek to articulate my position on a contemporary issue, I try to bring together two things: (1) a carefully researched understanding of the full conceptual framework and ethical principles that the Bible teaches, and (2) a thorough understanding of the full resources of modern thought (the social sciences, natural sciences, etc.). The Bible is my authority for faith and practice (for theology and ethics). But the Bible does not talk about whether we should build nuclear reactors or keep the comatose on life-support systems for years. To answer those questions, we have to combine biblical principles with sophisticated contemporary social and scientific analysis.

1. *Our environmental crisis.* The crisis is real and urgent. We must change not only our actions but our beliefs. Even secular people like Carl Sagan have begun pleading with the religious community to get involved. But what religious ideas will truly help us?

Some people are turning to varieties of Eastern monism. New Age adherents like the actress Shirley MacLaine say the solution is monism, which teaches that all is divine. But notice a couple of things. First of all, if monism is right and all is divine, then all is good and you cannot even distinguish between good and evil. Furthermore, the ideal in

Eastern monism is to escape this material world, turn within, and merge with the all. The material world is an illusion. The ideal is to merge with the Divine All in the way a drop of water falls into the ocean and disappears. The individual person loses all individual identity.

How does that worldview offer a solution to our environmental crisis? If the material world is an illusion, why worry about it?

Biblical faith is radically different. You and I and all the world around us are not divine. But we are very important. We are the creation of an all-powerful, all-loving Creator. We are finite but good. The material world is so good that the God of the universe, the Creator of 120 billion galaxies, became flesh on this little blue planet. The material world is so good that Jesus Christ rose bodily from death. The material world is so good that Jesus Christ promises to return to this earth and complete the victory over injustice, evil, and death itself.

Some environmentalists say persons are no more important than monkeys or moles or mushrooms. To claim a special status for the people is specieism. But if that is true, then civilization collapses. We have no right to eat anything or use anything in the world around us. Nor is redivinizing the material world the answer. In the film *Out of Africa,* the animists say they cannot build a dam because the water spirits live at the sea. That prevents wise use of the material world to improve human civilization.

The biblical view is a carefully balanced view. Persons alone are created in the image of God, and persons have the special task of being God's stewards over the rest of creation on this planet. But the Genesis story that talks about this says persons are to "care for" God's garden. The word actually means "to serve it."

The Bible also says the nonhuman creation has independent worth and significance entirely apart from you and me. The heavens declare the glory of God. The sun, moon, and stars sing praises to their Creator. The Creator cares about every endangered species. So we should too.

Christians have often neglected this full biblical teaching on the creation. And we have, along with Enlightenment naturalists, helped destroy the environment. For that, I repent. But I believe biblical faith offers a far better foundation for lovingly caring for this gorgeous creation than does Eastern monism, goddess worship, animism, or naturalism.

2. *Our inner cities.* I lived in one of the most desperate parts of Philadelphia for seven years. The violence, drug abuse, unemployment, and family chaos is almost unbelievable. And the causes are complex: racism; global economic forces that moved jobs to Third World countries; wrong personal choices about drugs, sex, and alcohol.

How do we solve it? The government has been trying to do that for decades. It has spent hundreds of billions of dollars on well-intentioned programs to renovate housing, provide Head Start, improve schools, and so on. A few things have helped. But the problems get worse and worse. Biblical faith says we have missed half of the problem. For wholeness, people need both a good external environment and internal integrity grounded in a right relationship to God.[12]

Let me tell you two stories. James Dennis is one of my special friends. For several years we served together as elders in an inner-city church. Thirty years ago James Dennis was an angry black militant. He hated whites. A few years ago, he said that if he had met me back then, he might have killed me. Thank God, he met Jesus first! Like so many inner-city young men with few decent job opportunities, James became an alcoholic. His marriage was in trouble, and he landed in prison for a serious crime. While there, someone shared the gospel with him, and he began to experience the transforming grace of Jesus Christ. When he left prison, our pastor walked beside him, supporting and discipling, and James became an active member and then an elder in our church. James Dennis is a radically different person today. He is still a proud African American who will not tolerate even the hint of white racism, but God erased his racial hatred and restored his family. He has a good job and owns his own home. Transforming grace has invaded his life.

Anybody who thinks that the best government programs for jobs, housing, and prison reform would have been enough to solve James Dennis's problems simply doesn't get it. He needed a personal relationship with Jesus Christ, which has transformed the core of his being, his values, inner convictions, and family life. At the same time, anybody who thinks that being born again, by itself, would have been enough to solve his problems doesn't get it either. James Dennis can be as born again as you like, but if the inner-city school system offers his children a lousy education, if decent housing is unavailable and there are no jobs to be found, he still has big problems.

For ten years, Raleigh Washington was the African American pastor of Rock of Our Salvation Church (Evangelical Free), an inner-city, interracial congregation on the west side of Chicago. Intimately connected with the church is Circle Urban Ministries, a holistic community center led by Glen Kehrein, a white farm boy from Wisconsin. Circle has a medical clinic with seven full-time doctors, a legal clinic with two full-time lawyers, a low-income housing program that has renovated millions of dollars of housing for the poor, and job-creation programs and small-business development to build an economic base in the inner city. But the community center staff know that unless they offer more than excellent medical or legal help, they will never get to the heart of the problems and produce lasting change. So when they sense a spiritual need, doctors and lawyers feel free to speak of Christ—or encourage the person to arrange a visit to one of the three chaplains who now work both in the community center and the church. The result has been a rapidly growing inner-city congregation with about five hundred members.

Some years ago, Cassandra Holmes Franklin came to Rock/Circle's medical clinic seeking a doctor's help. She got that, but the workers there also told her about Jesus. Soon she came to Christ, joined Rock Church, and started singing in the choir. A little later she married Showen, the father of her two children, who also soon came to personal faith. Now her husband has a job as partner in an economic development venture of Circle Ministries starting a small business. In a recent year his business had twelve employees and cleared a profit of $50,000. Jesus' kind of Christianity works! Rock/Circle is just one of hundreds of examples of committed Christian congregations daring to live and work in the midst of the agony of our inner cities in order to provide a holistic solution. Of course the government has a crucial role to play. There must be quality schools, decent housing, and above all, jobs that pay a living wage. But unless people are changed, unless racism is overcome in our hearts, unless our families are restored, the best government programs will fail.

3. *Family and feminism.* Everybody knows the American family is a disaster area. Social scientists regularly report the sad fact that children from homes where parents are divorced do more poorly in school, are more likely to get into crime, and so on. Furthermore, our society experiences incredible levels of rape, incest, and all kinds of sexual and physical violence against women.

The answer is not some kind of conservative religious patriarchy in which the husband dominates the home, ruling wife and children as lord and master. In fact, that kind of patriarchy probably contributes to sexual abuse in the home. But neither is the solution the kind of radical feminism that prefers lesbianism to marriage and places personal self-fulfillment above responsibility to children. I think biblical faith is just what we need. Jesus Christ, as we saw, was a feminist. He lived a radical challenge to the male chauvinists of his day, treating women as equals. The overarching principle that the apostle Paul spells out for husbands and wives in Ephesians 5 is mutual submission. Jesus calls men and women to sexual purity and joyful lifelong marriage covenant.

Let me put it personally. My wife, Arbutus, and I have been married for thirty-eight years. We believe in full mutuality in our marriage. We make our decisions together. We love sex, even at sixty, but we have never had sex with anyone else. There have been times in our marriage when we have hurt each other and struggled. We needed six months of marriage counseling once. But we were and are committed to each other for life, so we worked through those difficulties to a time of even greater joy and love. Our three children have never worried that we would get a divorce. We are both feminists—biblical feminists like Jesus, whom we love and worship.

I think the full biblical view of family, marriage, and the equality of women is what our aching homes need. You cannot have happy marriages if you screw around all through college and are never sure, even after marriage, if your partner will be faithful to you. Your marriage will not last if you see it as a limited contract that you will dissolve as soon as it does not feel good and fulfill your immediate personal needs. The demands for instant gratification and self-centered individualism are central causes of the hell that rampages through our marriages. There is a better way: the way that Jesus taught. It is possible—and in the long run full of greater joy and fulfillment—to reserve sex for marriage, to be faithful to your spouse. The full biblical view of family and feminism is just what this hurting society needs.

One final concluding point. Jesus teaches high standards. What happens when we fail? God—and the media—know Christians often do. Well, the cross of Jesus Christ is, I think, an astonishing answer. Christians believe that Jesus Christ took upon himself the punishment that our evil deeds deserve, so that a holy God could forgive our terrible acts against others and God.

The awful evil that you and I do to neighbors poses a terrible problem. Let me be personal. There was a period in our marriage when Arbutus and I hurt each other rather deeply. We could have said, "Aw, shucks, it doesn't matter. It was nothing. Forget it." That would have been pure nonsense. It hurt! Or we could have said, "That's it. I cannot forgive you." But then our relationship and the deep love we had shared for two decades would have ended. Instead, we did on a microcosmic scale what God did at the cross. Arbutus looked at me and said: "What you did was very evil. But I love you. I accept the pain of the evil you did to me, and I forgive you. Let's walk on together." I did the same for her. It wasn't easy, and it didn't happen in a day, month, or even a year. But the result has been renewed joy and wonderful happiness. According to the Bible sin is a terrible thing. It cannot be ignored. Hitlers and Stalins and wife beaters and liars and oppressors and rapists and racists all deserve punishment.

But at the cross, God, Jesus Christ who is very God, suffered the hell of Roman crucifixion because the Holy Creator combines justice and love in an awesome integration. God suffers the punishment you and I deserve so that evil deeds can be forgiven, so that broken people can be reconciled. The only alternative to divine and human forgiveness is an ever-widening circle of broken relationships, hostility, and violence. I don't pretend that evangelicals have always lived up to the high standards I have sketched. We have often failed to follow Jesus. But that is what we believe. And with the power of the risen Jesus in our lives, that is what we seek to live.

Why would anybody want to be an evangelical? First of all, because biblical faith is true. And second, because it works. If you don't believe me, I challenge you to examine the evidence—openly without bias. And then I dare you to try it.

6/
Higher Ground

Bryan A. Stevenson

He has showed you, O man, what is good.
     And what does the LORD require of you?
To act justly and to love mercy
     and to walk humbly with your God.
                        —Micah 6:8, NIV

AN IMPRISONED MURDERER who has admitted killing, attacking, and persecuting a lot of innocent people now claims to be transformed completely by God. What would you do if he asked you to help him to avoid being lawfully executed for his crimes? Would you question the sincerity of his newfound faith? Let's say his name is Saul, although he now prefers Paul, and he writes you amazing letters full of divine insight about faith and life as a *believer* of Jesus Christ. Would you support his effort to stay alive because of his extraordinary faith? Would his salvation make him reborn in a way that justified stopping his execution? Would you help him because of *your* faith? If your own faith prompted you to offer aid, would it matter whether the condemned was now a Christian or distinct in any way from other death row prisoners? Would God care if you chose to ignore his plea for help?

Seventeen years ago I found myself struggling with these questions. I was a law student who had agreed to spend a month in Georgia lending assistance to lawyers who provide legal aid to death row prisoners. I had been motivated to go to Georgia because the work would involve the kind of complex litigation skills I sought. I understood that bias against the poor and people of color contributed to the unfairness and injustice of capital punishment, and consequently I believed that this experience would be engaging and meaningful. However, I cannot honestly say that I had fully integrated my faith and my work until I found myself in the dark, dank corner of a prison in Jackson, Georgia.

The Georgia Diagnostic and Classification Center is where death row prisoners are housed and with increasing frequency executed. I had just completed a legal visit with a man on death row who had told me that I was the first person to visit him in over three years. He was overjoyed to see me. When I arrived he asked me to pray with him. He prayed earnestly and with great emotion, thanking God for sending him someone who would help. He grabbed my hands several times during the visit, and he cried a lot about his difficulties on death row and the pain and anguish he had caused before his arrest. He told me that he had been born again on death row and that he believed one day God would set him free. Our visit was abruptly ended by two prison guards who said our time was up. My new friend hugged me before the guards began shackling his feet. He grimaced as they handcuffed him tightly, and then he began to sing:

> *I'm pressing on the upward way,*
> *New heights I'm gaining every day;*
> *Still praying as I'm onward bound,*
> *Lord, plant my feet on higher ground.*

He smiled at me while he sang. As the guards shoved him out of the cell, he continued to sing. I could hear him as he shuffled down the long prison corridor:

Lord, lift me up and let me stand,
By faith on heaven's tableland;
A higher plane than I have found;
Lord, plant my feet on higher ground.

I wanted to leave the prison, but I sank down in the corner of the visitation room overwhelmed. Sometimes when God calls you it is as if there is a ringing in your spirit. You know that if you respond it is not what you say that will matter, it is what you do. In that prison on that day, I thought of the apostle Paul for the first time as a confessed killer. It became clear to me with devastating forcefulness that each of us is more than the worse thing that we have ever done. I understood in a radically new way that if you tell a lie, you are not just a liar; if you take something that doesn't belong to you, you are not simply a thief; that even if you kill someone, you are more than just a killer. As a sinner saved by grace, I don't know why this came to me as such a revelation, but it did.

For the last seventeen years I have provided legal representation and aid to death row prisoners in the Deep South. I have come to believe that while some Christians are called to preach, all Christians are called to serve. You find holiness in service, you find redemption in service, you find love through service, you find God in service. Not all of the people I represent are like the man I met in Georgia years ago. Some of my clients are very angry, disturbed, and confused. Many are mentally disabled. I have come to believe that my faith requires me to stand with the condemned regardless of their faith. Yet there are many believers on death row who minister to me as I provide legal assistance to them. It is an odd community of faith.

When I was a student of Tony Campolo at Eastern College, I would not have imagined that one day I would be connected to a faith community that is barred from stained glass churches, forced to congregate in windowless prison chambers. The core members of my community are the rejected and reviled, the hated and forgotten, the lowest of the low, the "least of them." I am often called to speak about these men, women, and children, not from a pulpit, but in a courtroom. Still, the message remains the same: I argue for hope on behalf of those who are perceived as hopeless. I seek redemption for those who are regarded as unredeemable, I advocate for life over death, and I pray for peace and mercy for all who are touched by the tragedy these cases reveal.

Currently there are 3,700 people on death row in the United States, and thirty-eight of the fifty states have death penalty statutes. Since the death penalty was resurrected in 1976,[1] there have been more than six hundred executions, most of which have been in the South. Women, juveniles, and the mentally ill are among the hundreds who have been shot, electrocuted, asphyxiated, and injected with lethal poisons by state governments in America. Most of these executions have taken place in the last ten years when support for capital punishment has generated greater political resonance and federal courts have retreated from the kind of oversight and review that existed in the early 1980s. In the last year of the twentieth century, the world's "leading democracy" executed close to one hundred of its residents. All of the executed were poor and a disproportionately high number were racial minorities with crime victims who were white. Many of the executed were mentally ill and some were juveniles at the time their crimes occurred. Further, there is no meaningful assurance that all of the executed were guilty of the crimes for which they had been convicted.

In the life of Jesus, I see God continually offering condemned people paths of redemption. I'm convinced that people of faith are required to do the same—not just for death row prisoners, but for everyone. However, to effectively challenge the demand to be tough and vengeful, which is so pervasive in our culture, we have to understand the larger realities that fuel the fear, anger, and alienation so many in our society feel.

The prevalence of violent crime in American society is overwhelming. There is so much heartbreaking, senseless violence. You don't have to be in any particular part of the country to appreciate how vexing the problem has become. Many of us feel a need to prepare our hearts before we read the newspaper or watch the news because we know we will be confronted with something ugly, something horrible, something debilitating to our very spirit. The pain of violent crime and the anguish associated with criminal behavior has made many angry and punitive. I see this anger and intense desire to punish not only in death penalty cases but in a variety of contexts.

Over the last twenty-five years tougher sentencing practices in the United States have resulted in an unprecedented increase in incarceration rates and have cost billions of dollars in increased spending related to prisons. The United States locks up its citizens at a rate five to ten times greater than that of most industrialized nations. The American prison population has increased from 200,000 in 1972 to 2 million in 2000. To keep pace with the explosion in the number of prisoners, federal and state governments are building prisons at an alarming rate. In 1999 the cost of building and operating prisons in the United States reached $40 billion. In many states, governments will spend more money on the operation of prisons than on public schools and education. For economic reasons, investing billions of dollars in correctional facilities and prison beds necessarily commits American society to maintaining the unprecedented level of incarceration of its citizens, regardless of decreases in crime rates.

Women and racial minorities have been most affected by these developments. There was a 400 percent increase in the number of women behind bars from 1980 to 1995. Today nearly a third of African American males between the ages of eighteen and thirty are in jail, prison, or under the supervision of the criminal justice system.

I currently represent a man named Jerald Sanders. He is one of thousands of nonviolent offenders in the United States who has been sentenced to life imprisonment without parole. Mr. Sanders is an indigent black man who has never committed a violent crime. He was sentenced under Alabama's habitual offender statute after he was convicted of stealing a bicycle from a porch in Mobile, Alabama. The state is spending close to $20,000 a year to keep Mr. Sanders imprisoned for the rest of his life for a property crime involving a $60 bike. Many states now sentence nonviolent offenders to life imprisonment without parole for petty crimes under habitual offender statutes. The fact that Mr. Sanders has become a devout Christian who lovingly and prayerfully gives to less fortunate prisoners around him means nothing in the law. He belongs to the growing caste of condemned human beings for whom change, rehabilitation, and redemption are legally meaningless.

There is something surreal about the way a civilized society can ignore, marginalize, and devastate whole segments of the human community. The closer you examine how the hope and humanity of so many are crushed by a commitment to be tough on crime the more distressing it becomes.

Years ago I received a call from a man who was thirty days away from a scheduled execution. He did not have legal assistance, his lawyers had told him there was nothing they could do. He asked me to represent him, but I explained that we did not have the resources to take on any additional cases. He hung up the phone sadly. It was an unsettling conversation for me. The next day he called again. He said, "Mr. Stevenson, I know you don't have the resources to represent me, and I know that I shouldn't continue to ask, but please tell me you'll help me. You don't have to tell me that you can block my execution, you don't have to tell me that you can obtain a stay, but please tell me that you'll fight for me with whatever you have." He continued by saying, "I don't think I can make it these next twenty-nine days if there is no hope at all." After speaking with him, I found it impossible to say no. My colleagues and I got involved and worked very hard to block his execution. We did not succeed. On the night his execution was scheduled, I received a call from the United States Supreme Court informing me that his last appeal had been denied. I drove to Atmore, Alabama, to be with this man before his scheduled execution and found the experience devastating. We prayed, cried, and shared together in those last moments.

We had a conversation that I have never forgotten. He told that me that all day prison guards had asked what they could do to help him. He said, "All day people have asked me what can I get you to eat? Do you need stamps to mail your last letters? Do you need access to the phone to call your friends and loved ones? Do you need coffee or water? What can I do to help you?" I will never forget him saying to me, "Bryan, it's been so strange, because more people have asked me what they can do to help in the last fourteen hours than they ever did in the first nineteen years of my life." As I stood there with this man, I couldn't avoid thinking where were these people when he was three years old and he was being physically abused by his parent? Where were they when he was six and he was being sexually abused by a step-parent? Where were they when he was nine and he was experimenting with crack cocaine? Where were they when he was fourteen, drug-addicted, homeless, and roaming the streets of Birmingham, Alabama, with no place to go? With these questions resonating in my mind, this man was pulled away from me and executed.

With some notable exceptions, most people of faith have been largely silent about the use of capital punishment and harsher sentencing in the United States. Many church communities have members who share the fear, anger, and frustration of violent crime that is pervasive in American society. In the fall of 1999 Alabama had a referendum on establishing the state's first lottery. The money generated by the lottery was to be used to improve the state's underfunded education system. A coalition of churches and religious groups banded together in opposition to the lottery. Billboards that read, "The Lottery: What Would Jesus Do?" went up all over the state, and in a surprising result, the lottery referendum was defeated. A few weeks after the referendum vote, our legal project decided to put billboards around Montgomery, Alabama, that read: "The Death Penalty: What Would Jesus Do?" At the bottom of the billboards we quoted John 8:7, where Jesus says to those who would stone a woman to death for her crimes, "Let him who is without sin cast the first stone." We asked area churches to join us in posting more billboards and initiating a campaign that would challenge people of faith to think more critically about capital punishment and the treatment of the imprisoned. We got very little support. Some church leaders were even antagonized and angry about our billboards. There clearly was great discomfort around our invocation of the ever-popular, ubiquitous WWJD? in the context of capital punishment.

Despite all that we believe about forgiveness, God's mercy, and the call to be just and compassionate, many of us struggle with how to treat those who have committed crimes. On crime issues Americans have generally become much less forgiving in the last fifteen years. For example, the United States leads the world in executing juvenile offenders. Of the six countries known to have executed juvenile offenders since 1990,[2] only the United States executed juvenile offenders last year.

Seventy juvenile offenders are currently being held on death row in America.[3] The trend toward executing younger children in the United States seems to get worse each year. Last year in the state of Alabama, nearly 50 percent of those sentenced to death were nineteen years old or younger. Of the forty jurisdictions that have statutes authorizing the death penalty, four states have set the minimum age of eligibility for a death sentence at seventeen, and twenty states use age sixteen as the minimum age.[4] In light of recent increases in violent juvenile crime, some political leaders have proposed legislation under which children as young as eleven could be sentenced to death.

Discrimination on the basis of race is particularly egregious among juvenile offenders. Seventy-five percent of juvenile offenders executed in the United States have been people of color, while nearly 90 percent of the victims in these cases were white. Of the nine girls executed in United States history, eight were African American and one was Native American. Today juvenile death sentences are given much more frequently to African Americans and Latinos than to whites. Of those sentenced to death for crimes committed as juveniles, nearly two-thirds are African American.

I frequently go into low-income communities and find myself talking with young thirteen and fourteen-year-old black and Latino boys who are fully aware of their diminishing status in a society that unapologetically executes the children it loves the least. Many of these kids tell me that they don't believe that they will live past the age of eighteen. They say, "Don't talk to me about staying in school, Mr. Stevenson. I'm going to be dead by the time I'm eighteen, so I gotta get mine while I can." They don't say these things because of what they see on TV or what they have heard; they say these things because they see their siblings, friends, and relatives dying as teenagers from drugs, gun violence, and gang activity, or in effect dying by being sent to prison for the rest of their lives. A number of policy issues are implicated by the despair and dysfunction that have led these young people to such a bleak and dreadful place, but ultimately these are kids who suffer from a profound absence of hope. Without resurrecting hope for these children, no policy initiative will succeed in creating a different future than the one they imagine.

Children with mental illness or retardation are in particular jeopardy. A 1988 study of fourteen juvenile offenders sentenced to death revealed that all had suffered head injuries as children and had serious psychiatric problems. Twelve of these boys had been beaten, whipped, or otherwise physically abused; five had been sodomized by older male relatives. Only two had IQ scores above ninety, and three did not learn to read at all until they reached death row. Nine boys showed serious neurological abnormalities, including brain damage, seizures, or unusual brain-wave patterns. All suffered from mental illness—seven were psychotic, four had a history of severe mood disorder, and the other three had periodic paranoid ideation,[5] yet only five received any psychiatric evaluation before their trials.[6]

Histories of severe abuse, mental illness, and retardation are not unique to juveniles on death row. Despite the Supreme Court's mandate that mental disorders must be presented to juries as mitigating factors, thirty-four adults and juvenile offenders known to be mentally retarded have been executed in the United States to date. The American public and twelve states have recently opposed capital punishment for the mentally retarded, but more than three hundred people known to be retarded currently await execution on death row.[7]

Mental illness among those sentenced to death is prevalent but likewise tends to go undetected. The Supreme Court held in 1986 that the insane cannot be executed, but this decision protects only "those who are unaware of the punishment they are about to suffer and why they are to suffer it.[8] Mentally ill and retarded defendants who display even fleeting or minimal comprehension are considered "death eligible." [9]

The poor and people of color are also at great risk. It is frequently said that in the United States "capital punishment means them without the capital gets the punishment." Sadly, the U.S. criminal justice system works much better for the rich and guilty than the poor and innocent. Much has been written about capital trials in the United States where defense attorneys were asleep, intoxicated, publicly stating a belief that their client should be executed, directing racial slurs at the client, or otherwise providing ineffective assistance of counsel.[10] Hundreds of death row prisoners in the United States currently have no legal representation and dim prospects of finding counsel. With no constitutional right to counsel, people on death row cannot effectively file appeals that have frequently proved vital in demonstrating innocence or otherwise establishing that a conviction or sentence is illegal.[11]

Bias against the poor is exacerbated by bias against racial minorities. The imposition of the death penalty in the United States continues to reveal an insidious race consciousness. Of the 3,700 people currently on death row, more than half are people of color: 46.48 percent are white, 42.53 percent are black, 8.39 percent are Latino, and 1.35 percent are Native Americans. Examining the statistics for some states reveals an even bleaker picture. In Pennsylvania 83 percent of people sent to death row from Philadelphia are African American. Strikingly, of the five hundred people executed between 1976—the year the U.S. Supreme Court permitted the reinstatement of the death penalty—and the end of 1998, 81 percent were convicted for the murder of a white person despite the fact that about half of all U.S. murder victims are black. In the southern states of Alabama, Georgia, and Mississippi, two-thirds of those executed have been black.

The problems created by so much discrimination, injustice, and unfairness are overwhelming and debilitating. To respond effectively to this bleak picture you must have more than good ideas and reform strategies in your mind; you must have some conviction in your heart. You have to have a hope that is grounded. A whimsical preference for optimism over pessimism or some naive expectation that things will get better will not suffice. Rather, your hope has to be an orientation of the spirit, a willingness to position yourself in the face of despair because you recognize that your presence and witness represent hope.

I believe people of faith need to have a vision of justice when confronted with evidence of injustice. We must offer our legal system a way of reconciliation and redemption. Without a new vision, the fear and anger we see and feel around us, and even within us, is going to get worse. We have to combat the hopelessness by finding ways, not only to preach forgiveness and reconciliation for those who hurt us, but to step in and catch the stones of condemnation cast by others. We need a desire for justice that energizes us, a compassion for the broken and rejected among us that empowers and heals. We need a faith that allows us to forgive those who have grieved us and seek forgiveness from those we have hurt. But, as servants, we also need an extra measure of grace. Grace will allow us to step forward and seek forgiveness for and from those who don't want to become agents of God's forgiveness. Only by stepping out to catch some of the stones of condemnation that have been cast do we make the promise, the hope, and the glory of Christ real in the lives of desperately alienated people.

This is our mission. This is our calling.

When we think about making such a vision of redemption a reality, we are really addressing what it means to trust and believe God's promise. Without an abiding faith in God's redemptive power, we will never make it through the challenges that face us. In dealing with the intimidating injustice of the criminal system—or with injustice anywhere—we need to have a faith-filled vision like that of Isaiah. We need to believe that every valley—valleys where hopelessness, despair, and degradation have triumphed—can be raised up and exalted. We have to believe that the high places—the mountains of condemnation and discrimination—can be made low. We must be convinced that the crooked paths that keep us from reconciliation can be made straight and the rough places of anger and vengeance can be made plain. Without such a faith, we really cannot sustain the work to which God calls us.

We must not avoid the difficulty of our situation. Justice is a constant struggle; often where there is no struggle there is likely to be no justice. Our work has to be cognizant of the sobering realities that shape the way our society functions. We need a faith rooted in the Christ whose life demonstrates that truth crushed to earth will rise again. An active, abiding faith is necessary in responding to the problems of injustice, the absence of hope, and the desire to avenge rather than forgive.

I have come to truly appreciate a lot more about faith-based, social justice struggle working in Montgomery, Alabama. There is a rich history of inspired activism in Montgomery that is still energizing to those who understand it. My appreciation for the costly sacrifices of the people who led the civil rights movement in the 1950s and 1960s has grown as I've been here. Driving around Montgomery, I realize that the city is far more sprawling than I had imagined when I first heard of the bus boycotts of 1955.

The Montgomery bus boycott lasted almost a year before it led to changes in the segregated busing system. Domestic workers walked miles every day to their places of employment and back home again. During the struggle, many became tired and weary. After several months, some began to suggest it was time to end the boycott. They feared they would never prevail. The problem was perceived to be too big. A handful of people trying to preach to a hostile or indifferent world that racial segregation was wrong, sinful, and unjust could never succeed. It was too much to ask. As time went on, the movement to end the boycott became stronger.

One night at a mass meeting in the eighth or ninth month, it looked as if the boycott was sure to end. Younger people in the movement argued that the cost of boycotting buses for so long was too great. It wasn't fair to older African Americans in the community who were struggling to walk to and from work each day. It was time to realize that being in the back of the bus was better than not being on the bus at all. When there seemed to be growing support for this view, an older woman got up and made her way to the front of the church. "Don't stop nothin' for me," she said. "I'm going to keep on walking, because I've got a vision. Yes, I'm tired, but I believe that one day I'm going to sit on the front seat of a bus in Montgomery, and I'm not going to stop walking until it happens." She concluded, "My feet are tired, but my soul is rested. Because my soul is rested, I believe I can walk on a while longer."

We know what it is like to feel tired. We are weary of trying to bring hope and reconciliation to communities that seem hopeless and irreconcilable. We know that many people are disbelieving when we talk about rehabilitation for those who have committed serious crime. Some laugh when we talk about mercy or justice. Some shrug their shoulders when we talk about a society and a legal system that do not discriminate on the basis of race. People scoff when we talk about a world where poverty doesn't undermine the aspirations of so many. Yet we have this hope, a hope rooted in Christ. That hope gives us the strength to keep walking, to move forward, to do the work to which God has called us.

I feel quite privileged to be involved in work that can be restorative and to see grace triumph over condemnation. However, it's hard to feel special. All around us are opportunities to reach out to the marginalized and broken, the imprisoned and despairing, the forgotten and discarded. In my work we have succeeded in winning new trials and reduced sentences for dozens of death row prisoners who were unfairly convicted or sentenced. My colleagues and I have been blessed to win the release of innocent people wrongly convicted and sentenced to death for crimes they did not commit. However, for me nothing has been more energizing and empowering than to see rejected men, women, and children recover enough hope and faith to press on the upward way, to gain new heights and pray, "Lord, plant my feet on higher ground."

7/
From Protest to Covenant

Jim Wallis

IN 1995, REPUBLICANS and Democrats were locked in a bitter political confrontation regarding what to do about poverty in America. Yet that welfare reform debate offered a false choice between unsatisfactory alternatives. In order to meet their goals of spending and tax cuts, conservative Republicans ended up targeting the poorest and most vulnerable citizens to bear the brunt of deficit reduction, while trying to loyally preserve "corporate welfare" for agribusiness and Wall Street. The Democrats also failed to offer any real alternatives to the welfare system. Time and time again they bypassed opportunities to reform the system, failing to see that large and distant bureaucracies have too often created more dependency than opportunity, more control than caring, and more wasteful inefficiency than personal and family success. Wedded to old approaches and vested constituencies, the Democrats had long been mere defenders of the status quo.

On December 7, 1995, as the welfare and budget bills were being debated, evangelical pastors, Catholic priests, and inner-city church workers from around the country (including Tony Campolo and I) entered the rotunda of the U.S. Capitol to proclaim a prophetic biblical word and to pray for the poor in the face of their assailants. We offered more than a protest; we gave an invitation. We were all deeply involved in our local communities to create the new approaches the nation sorely needs. We not only called for an alternative vision, but actually represented it.

We knelt and prayed for the poor of our neighborhoods and called the nation's political leaders to repentance—to seek new solutions together, to find common ground, and to protect the poor—recognizing the Bible's insistence that the best test of a nation's righteousness is how it treats the poorest and most vulnerable in its midst.

Together we testified that a fundamentally new approach to the alleviation of poverty in America is critically needed. But we also clearly stated that it was absolutely immoral, from a Christian perspective, to slash and burn systems and safety nets without offering anything to replace them.

After proclaiming in a strong unison voice the words of Isaiah 10:1-2—

> Woe to the legislators of infamous laws,
> to those who issue tyrannical decrees,
> who refuse justice to the unfortunate
> who cheat the poor among my people of their rights,
> who make widows their prey
> and rob the orphan. (Jerusalem Bible)

we were arrested in the rotunda and taken to jail, but our point was made.

It was the first time Tony had been arrested in a civil disobedience action, and as he told the judge at our hearing: "What seems to be at stake in the present discussion on the budget is a whole redefinition of what government is supposed to be and do. The Bible says that the government was ordained by God to do the good of God (Romans 13). And I believe that the extreme action that I took on December 7 was an attempt to call the government back to this biblically prescribed responsibility."[1]

In the holding cell that afternoon, a vision was born. While waiting to be processed, the entire group discussed the urgent need to create approaches and strategies that are community based, locally focused, value centered, family building, job creating, and solution oriented. These solutions cannot depend just on government programs, which the Democrats have preferred, nor can they simply "dump" the problem onto churches and charities as Republican leaders have suggested.

In contrast to both liberal and conservative approaches, fresh solutions must involve partnerships among nonprofit community organizations (both religious and non-religious), the business sector, private foundations, and government on all levels. If they hope to be successful, new configurations in the "civil society" must create strategies and mobilize resources, both public and private.

This new approach will depend on everyone's involvement. It will call for increased volunteer activity from every sector of the society—drawing on both the energy of young people and the expertise of older generations. It will demand that businesses take much more responsibility for the communities in which they work and profit. It will need the strategic and collaborative investment of private foundations on national, regional, and local levels. And, it will require the active engagement of government—federal, state, and local—although perhaps in different ways.

Private-public partnerships must shape the strategies that will work for each community and then make sure that the resources are there to accomplish the necessary tasks. Because of their vocation to cultivate moral leadership and their presence throughout the country, churches and religious communities can play a catalytic role in developing and convening such new partnerships and strategies. Indeed, they must.

Change—fundamental change—is desperately needed in our approach to the complex of issues around poverty: the failures of the welfare system itself; the social disintegration of family and community; the corporate downsizing, loss of jobs, and decline in real wages in a changing global economy; and the assaults upon positive personal and social values in the popular culture. These factors combine to devastate the lives of poor people, especially children.

In the years since that day in December 1995, the new movement we envisioned in a jail cell has been born. Call to Renewal has gone from a dream to a biblically based federation of churches and faith-based organizations committed to overcoming poverty in our country. We have convened four meetings of a "Christian Roundtable on Poverty and Welfare Reform" that have brought together the leaders of a broad spectrum of the church in America—from the National Association of Evangelicals to the National Council of Churches, from the U.S. Catholic Conference to the Salvation Army, from the Progressive National Baptist Convention to the Family Research Council, from World Vision to the Christian Community Development Association. We have also held four national conferences bringing together hundreds of local pastors and faith-based organizations for networking, education, and inspiration. We have prayed together and talked about our common principles as Christians and how those principles could lead to policies for overcoming poverty.

These efforts have helped to create new networks of cooperation among churches and faith-based organizations at the local and national levels. We have helped to build partnerships with other faith traditions, nonprofit organizations, and business, labor, and government officials. We are tuning a unified faith-based and nonpartisan voice on the most critical public issues that affect people who are poor, and indeed, that might shape a more fair and just society for us all.

The emergence of the term "faith-based organization" (FBO) in political discussion may signal one of the most significant new developments in American public life. The pioneering efforts of faith communities are finding real solutions to the poverty and violence in many local communities around the country. Two of the most powerful forces in the country today are service and spirituality. The growing evidence of both is visible almost everywhere, and together they provide the most potent combination for changing our communities. They are growing streams of committed energy, which, as they begin to flow together, are creating a mighty river of action.

This so-called spiritual politics is forging new solutions in local communities across the country by developing civic projects and partnerships committed not just to alleviating the effects of poverty but to actually overcoming it. The devolution of national social policy from the federal to the local level will only strengthen the role of religious communities. While FBOs have long provided the bulk of the nation's social volunteer force, now their successes are being explored by politicians and social policy analysts searching for new answers.

But if FBOs are indeed "invited to the table," their role will not be simply to make government more efficient, but to make America more just. Their task will not be just to clean up the mess created by bad social policy or to take the place of legitimate government responsibilities, but to be a morally prophetic voice calling for new policies.

In this partnership, we will raise the common moral values on which our society must build, and insist on a strong standard of the common good to guide public policy. We will argue that the development of public policy must not be dictated merely by the clash of power and competing interests, but also by fundamental questions of right and wrong—questions asking what our moral vision is, what kind of people we want to be, and what kind of country we want to have.

Today an incredibly vibrant "direct citizen" political movement is occurring in many local communities. Much of it is tied to nonprofit institutions, among them many FBOs. National politics must wake up to this movement and begin to connect with all of its grassroots energy and innovation. Perhaps we are at the beginning of that recognition as more and more political leaders are showing interest in FBOs. There is enormous potential here—not just for a few exemplary programs, but for a new vision of real social change. It's a strategy that goes beyond Left and Right, Republican and Democrat, that engages the grassroots. Best of all, it is a strategy that might really work. We must learn how to make the connections between spirituality and politics, while vigorously protecting First Amendment rights of religious freedom.

Now, as we enter the twenty-first century, we hear about each new record-breaking milestone in the booming economy, while each new study tells us alarming facts on child poverty. When the NASDAQ reaches an all time high, politicians take the credit, but when we hear that poor families are still stuck at the bottom of the socioeconomic ladder, who takes the credit—or blame—then? Inflation and unemployment are at all time lows, but the food banks and soup kitchens report growing needs from hungry people. America is enjoying unprecedented prosperity, but not all Americans are sharing in the good life. The rising tide is lifting all the yachts, but not yet all the boats. The welfare rolls are certainly down, but many of the welfare poor have simply become the working poor. And, many of the families showing up in all the new poverty statistics are women and children.

Consider these statistics:

- Thirty million Americans worry about where they will get their next meal, according to a recent report by Tufts University Center on Hunger and Poverty. Nearly one in six children—over 12 million—lives in a household where hunger is a constant concern. Some families face a harsh choice: heat the home or feed the children. The Tufts study noted, "The strong economy is not reducing hunger, because even though more households are in the workforce, their take-home pay is not enough to feed their families."[2]

- Between 2.3 and 3.5 million Americans experience homelessness over the course of a year, according to findings by The Urban Institute. If we consider those Americans living in poverty, the likelihood of experiencing homelessness increases. And 25 percent of the homeless are children—an estimated 900,000 to 1.35 million of them.[3]

- Hunger and homelessness continue to grow in the nation's largest cities, according to the U.S. Conference of Mayors' most recent annual survey. Demand for emergency food assistance during 1999 grew by 18 percent over 1998, and an estimated 21 percent of those requests for food went unmet. Demand for emergency housing assistance grew by 12 percent since 1998, with families with children comprising 37 percent of those needing assistance.[4]

These statistics represent real people, real lives, but they don't tell the real stories of poverty.

Sojourners magazine assistant editor Rose Berger recently met a woman at a local Burger King. Rose was in the fast-food place eating french fries and writing in her journal when she noticed that the woman at the drive-through window kept running back and forth to a table in the corner where three young children were sitting. Soon Rose realized that these were the woman's children, and that she was trying to look after them and help them with their homework at 4 P.M.

at the Burger King. I call her "Burger King Mom" because she has become an icon for me of the new face of poverty in America today.

The saddest thing is that this woman is now put forward as the success story of welfare reform. Sure, she's working now, but she is likely poorer than when she was on welfare. Like many single mothers who can't get more than entry-level jobs, she has to make choices between rent, winter boots, and taking her kids to the doctor. Yet she's working hard and full time, "playing by the rules" as people say. Even across the political spectrum, most Americans would agree with the sound byte "People who work hard and full time shouldn't be poor." What churches and FBOs must do is put Burger King Mom's face and family before the American people. That indeed is the challenge Call to Renewal has taken on—putting poor people and their poverty on the national agenda, in both the secular and religious arenas.

Meanwhile, the income gap between the rich and poor in America continues to widen. Increasingly, our economic system is producing a society of extremes. Despite a record-breaking economy, the gap continues to grow between the top and bottom of the society. Virtually no one disputes that anymore. Even articles in *The Wall Street Journal* now agree with the familiar adage—"the rich get richer and the poor get poorer." The people at the top have received the lion's share of the economic windfall from the economic boom, the middle far less, and the bottom almost none at all.

As the stock market's Dow Jones average has climbed past the 10,000 mark, 42 percent of the benefits have gone to the top 1 percent of households and 86 percent of the benefits to the top 10 percent of households. Almost 90 percent of all stocks and mutual funds owned by households are held by the richest 10 percent.[5] The lowest fifth of American households have seen their real family income decrease 7 percent since 1979, while the top fifth has seen theirs increase 34 percent. The top 1 percent of society has increased its household income by 106 percent.[6]

Thirty years ago, the chief executive officers of most big companies made approximately 30 times what their average employees did. That 30 to 1 ratio still prevails today in places like Germany and Japan. But in the U.S., the ratio of CEO to average workers' salaries in America's largest companies is now 419 to 1, according to *Business Week*.[7]

This growing discrepancy means a huge difference in financial security. In the United States, the top 5 percent of the population now controls approximately 60 percent of the wealth, and the bottom 40 percent just 0.5 percent. And the top 1 percent of the population possesses a whopping 40 percent of all American wealth. Since the mid-1970s, the top 1 percent of households have doubled their share of the national wealth. Never have we seen such a radical redistribution of wealth from the bottom and the middle of society to the top.[8]

In this era of unprecedented prosperity and continued poverty, there are lessons we can learn from, of all things, biblical archeology. When the archeologists dig down into the ruins of ancient Israel, they find periods of time when the houses were more or less the same size and when the artifacts show a relative equality in the people's standard of living. During those periods the prophets were silent. They literally had nothing to say. No Isaiah, Amos, or Jeremiah could be heard. But digging into the ruins of other periods revealed the remains of very large houses and tiny hovels and the artifacts suggest great disparities of wealth among the people. Strikingly, it is during those periods that the prophets came to life, proclaiming the judgment and justice of God and calling the people to repentance. The prophets made clear that God would not endure such great and outrageous gaps between the haves and have-nots among God's people.

The only difference between those biblical periods and ours is that the inequities that prompted the ancient prophets to speak would pale in significance to the divisions between rich and poor that we accept as normal today. The 1998 U.N. Development Program report said that the world's three richest families now have more wealth than the world's 48 poorest countries.[9]

Overcoming poverty must become a nonpartisan issue and a bipartisan cause. Faith-based organizations are taking the lead in taking action on the issue. They are coming together in a way never seen before, partnering and strategizing to solve the problems of poverty—and they are calling political leaders to pay attention, to learn, and then to take action alongside the private sector.

Call to Renewal's work of the past years is now bearing fruit. At the fourth Roundtable discussion in December 1999, a "Covenant to Overcome Poverty" was developed. In that covenant, we proclaim:

The persistence of widespread poverty in our midst is morally unacceptable. Just as some of our religious forebears decided to no longer accept slavery or segregation, we decide to no longer accept poverty and its disproportionate impact on people of color. In the biblical tradition, we covenant together in a Call to Renewal. By entering this Covenant, we commit ourselves to:

1. Prioritize people who are poor—both in our personal, family, and vocational lives and in our congregational and organizational practices—through prayer and dedication of our time and resources.

2. Decide our financial choices in ways that promote economic opportunity and justice for those in poverty.

3. Evaluate public policies and political candidates by how they impact people who are poor.

4. Challenge racism, dismantle the structures of racial injustice and white privilege still present, and seek reconciliation among all groups in our society.

5. Nurture the bonds of family and community and protect the dignity of each person.

6. Organize across barriers of race, denomination, and social boundaries in common commitment and action to overcome poverty in our own communities, our nation, and our world.

This is not to overlook that the causes of poverty are complex. They include economic inequality, lack of opportunity, and institutional racism, as well as irresponsible personal choices and the breakdown of families and communities. The solutions to overcoming poverty are equally complex. Yet, we can overcome—but only if we act together and only if all sectors of society do what they do best. Call to Renewal's vision of a good social order is one where each sector makes its unique contribution to the common good.

Call to Renewal claims no detailed blueprint for overcoming poverty, but we believe that biblical norms and Christian reflection compel us to set forth practical goals that every sector in this society should work to accomplish. Specifically, we believe that a good society should achieve:

- A living family income for all who responsibly work. This should include an appropriate mix of a minimum wage/living income, Earned Income Tax Credit (EITC), and targeted help with child care, food, transportation, and housing. People who work full time should not be poor.
- Affordable, quality healthcare for all, regardless of income. It is unacceptable that 44 million Americans, including 11 million children, continue to lack health insurance.
- Schools that work for all children. We can no longer blur the moral issue that children's educational opportunities are unjustly based on where they live and their parents' income.
- Safe, affordable housing. Eliminating poverty housing and home-lessness through affordable housing must be a societal goal.
- Safe and secure neighborhoods. A safe and healthy environment is essential to rebuilding families and communities. We must elimi-nate crime and violence and end the scourge of life-destroying drugs.
- Family-friendly policies and programs in every sector of society. Strong families and communities must be rebuilt as the primary foundation and nurturing networks of a healthy society.
- Full participation by people of all races. We must embrace our diversity by having zero tolerance for racism and making racial justice and reconciliation a top national priority.

Each of these goals is a moral priority for members of Call to Renewal. How we achieve them should be a subject of a new dialogue among every sector of society. We are not committed to any particular ideological method or partisan agenda to achieve these goals—only that they be achieved. Partisan divisions and political disagreements have for too long prevented real solutions to poverty, and it is real solutions to which we must all commit ourselves. Overcoming pover-ty is our goal. We must together focus on how to accomplish that goal, but how we get there is less important than getting there.

A new unity around the issue of poverty in the religious community gives us the best opportunity in years to put it on the national political agenda. But doing so will require changing the direction of public discussion. Things will not change by just appealing to politicians who keep their wet fingers in the wind; we must change the wind.

When you begin to change the wind, the advocacy of particular measures which will make a real difference becomes much more possible. On this issue only a spiritual commitment will change the political will of the country, the atmosphere of the debate, and the public momentum around the issue of poverty. That's the kind of commitment other effective social movements have fostered, and a gathering momentum is now perceptible around the issue of poverty as previously divided churches come together.

Afterword/
He Came Our Way

John David Burton

Editor's Note: The following comments were gleaned from John David Burton's remarks during the February 2000 Eastern College chapel honoring Tony Campolo's sixty-fifth birthday.

JOHN DAVID BURTON WAS Tony Campolo's first mentor in pastoral ministry. Forty-seven years ago, when Tony was eighteen years old and a seminary student at Eastern Baptist Theological Seminary, he inquired about a internship at Burton's church, the First Presbyterian Church of Mount Holly, New Jersey. Pastor Burton brought Tony home to have a meal and to meet his wife. A relationship was begun that day. Tony worked as an intern at the church the next four years. Burton sensed a uniqueness about this young intern—a uniqueness epitomized in his reflection, "God danced on the day you were born."

Burton recalls a couple highlights of Tony's internship at First Presbyterian. One year, Tony and Pastor Burton cotaught a boxing class for ten- to twelve-year-old boys during a Vacation Bible School. Burton, a former Golden Gloves contender, reminisces, "We needed some way to work off the [kids'] energy." Burton also remembers asking Tony to read Scripture during a Sunday morning Mother's Day service. The selected text was 1 Corinthians 13. When Tony stepped to the pulpit, he inadvertently read a text from somewhere in 2 Corinthians, which dealt with fornicators and sexual immorality—no reference to love or anything remotely related to Mother's Day. After the service, the perplexed pastor spoke to the seemingly unaware new intern. "Tony," Pastor Burton remarked, "you read the Scripture very well this morning and with great passion, but it was the wrong passage!"

It is fitting that John David Burton, Tony Campolo's first mentor in ministry, has written this poetic afterword in Tony's honor.

> [Jesus asked,] "What did you go out into the wilderness to look at? A reed shaken by the wind?"
> —*Matthew 11:7*

> [Jesus said,] "By this everyone will know that you are my disciples, if you have love for one another."
> —*John 13:35*

> He came our way, a stripling twenty years old,
>   looking for all the world like a raw recruit
>   from the ranks of one of Caesar's legions.

> He came our way, young one in his search,
>   saying, "I want to learn by working in your church."
> So it was done, and later people
>   blessed the day he came our way.

> Now, in light of his present fame,
>   we would like to claim that we
>   shaped him into what he came to be.

> In truth, even then we could see that he had
>   the fire in his belly, a burning in his bones,

a lilt in his voice, a light in his eyes,
a lift in his step, love and laughter on his lips.

Long before he came our way, there was in him
steel to be honed by the church,
love for God and others to be
refined, defined by living,
All of what he has come to be was there
in embryo the day he came our way.

From coming our way, he has gone
the way Christ calls,
to be a beggar for Jesus and for
the poor whom Jesus loves.
In being scolded by left and right and others in between,
he meets the test his Master sets:
"Woe to you when all speak well of you, for that
is what their ancestors did to the false prophets."
                                                    —*Luke 6:26*

And now? Where to from here? Now that
good report is made of him, what more to do?
Why, what he and we knew long ago. The only
reward of good work is more good work to do.
He will continue burdening the comfortable
that they may comfort the burdened.
No doctrine may define him,
no theology take him in.
He says that loving sinners is God's
way of overcoming sin.

We leave him now to what God
has yet for him to do.
He came our way. When comes such another?

Endnotes

Chapter 1: Focus on the "Biblical Family"

1. The Nayar of India is an example of a family system arguably without a nuclear family unit.

2. Lewis Smedes, *Sex for Christians: The Limits and Liberties of Sexual Living*, rev. ed. (Grand Rapids: Eerdmans, 1994). See also Lewis Smedes, "Like the Wideness of the Sea," *Perspectives* 14, no. 5 (May 1999): 8-12.

3. The North American family system has a strong, mainstream ideological emphasis on the nuclear, monogamous, neolocal family system. Yet the diversity of cultural groups that live in Canada and the United States means we can empirically find instances of extended families, polygynous families, as well as matrifocal, matrilocal versions of traditional families found in other societies around the globe.

4. Emmanuel Todd, *The Explanation of Ideology: Family Structures and Social Systems* (Oxford: Blackwell, 1985).

5. For one thing, Todd excludes African family systems because of the large number of variables involved that make it more difficult to classify them. Thus, more work remains to be done on his typology.

6. Leviticus 17:8-9 speaks of the alien who offers a burnt offering or sacrifice but not to the Lord (and hence idolatrously); 17:10-16 deals with "eating blood"; 18:1-30 concerns the specific sexual immorality involved in marrying or having sexual relations with "near kin," spelling out what that means for both the Israelites and the aliens living among them. In this case, we have good reason for believing that the issues listed in the Jerusalem council decision had to do with facilitating fellowship between the two broad groups of Jewish and Gentile Christians and for supposing that "sexual immorality" refers specifically to rules of exogamy and incest. See Ernst Haenchen, *The Acts of the Apostles: A Commentary* (Oxford: Basil Blackwell, 1971), 449, n.4; Frederick F. Bruce, *The Acts of the Apostles: The Greek Text with Introduction and Commentary,* 3d rev. ed. (Grand Rapids: Eerdmans, 1990), 342-43. Johannes P. Louw and Eugene Nida, *Greek-English Lexicon of the New Testament Based on Semantic Domains, Vol. 1.: "Introduction and Domains"* (New York: United Bible Societies, 1988), 771, 88.271, say, "In some NT contexts *porneia* may refer specifically to incest."

7. For details on the meaning of Leviticus 18 and its terminology, see John E. Hartley, *Leviticus, Word Biblical Commentary* (Dallas: Word, 1992), 280-301. Anthropologists have noted a universal incest taboo found in all human cultures (though outside of parents and their own children the details of who is too close for comfort varies). What is striking is that Israel's vivid and almost "violent" language in refer-ring to these sorts of sexual relations treats these practices as violating something sacred. It reflects similar sensibilities found in most cultures. Israel's language ties incestuous relationships to notions of purity boundaries and the sense that some things violate the covenant rela-tionship at a more basic level than other matters. In addition, these matters are also identified as ways the Israelites are to distinguish their lifestyle from the corrupt customs and practices of Egypt and Canaan.

8. The most detailed examination of the levels of social organization that involved "family" ties is given by Norman Gottwald, *The Tribes of Yahweh: A Sociology of the Religion of Liberated Israel, 1250-1050 B.C.E.* (Maryknoll, N.Y.: Orbis, 1979), esp. pt. 4, pp. 237-41. But see also the writings of C. J. H. Wright, "Family," in David N. Freedman, ed., *Anchor Bible Dictionary* (New York: Doubleday, 1992), 2:761-69; *An Eye for An Eye* (Downers Grove, Ill.: InterVarsity Press, 1983); *God's People in God's Land* (Grand Rapids: Eerdmans, 1990).

9. Some of the following is based on the analysis of Bruce J. Malina, *The New Testament World: Insights from Cultural Anthropology* (Atlanta: John Knox, 1981), 105-18. For an account of kinship/marriage terminology, see Charles Taber, "Kinship and Marriage," in Keith Krim, ed., *The Interpreter's Dictionary of the Bible,* suppl. vol. (Nashville: Abingdon, 1976), 519-24.

10. We find preferential parallel cousin marriages within the patrilineage: Isaac marries his father's brother's daughter (Genesis 24:15); Jacob marries his mother's brother's daughters (Genesis 29:10), but Jacob's mother is, in this case, also a member of the patrilineage by descent from Abraham's brother; Esau married, among other wives, his father's brother's daughter, i.e., a granddaughter of Abraham (Genesis 28:9). When such a partner could not be found, other women from within the patrilineage would do: Abraham married his half-sister (Genesis 20:12); his brother Nahor married his brother's daughter—his niece (Genesis 11:29). There is also the case of Moses and Aaron's father marrying his father's sister (Exodus 6:60). Later rules consider some of these types of marriage as unsuitably close (incest).

11. See the account of the Herodian family marriages and divorces in K. C. Hanson and Douglas E. Oakman, *Palestine in the Time of Jesus: Social Structures and Social Conflicts* (Minneapolis: Fortress Press, 1998), 32-34, 44-46.

12. Wright, *An Eye for an Eye,* argues for the centrality of the family in the paradigm-type society Israel was to be. The family stands at the center of the other dominant elements: land, God, and society. The health and spiritual nature of the nation depended on the health of the family/household itself. Waldemar Janzen, *Old Testament Ethics: A Paradigmatic Approach* (Louisville: Westminster John Knox, 1994), argues something very similar. The family paradigm is the central controlling set of values and images that govern the basic core identity of Israel. Familial values of life, land, and hospitality get transposed into the kingdom theology of Jesus and into the household of God in the New Testament.

13. Jewish thought recognized the legal category of "concession." Jesus reminds them of this while appealing to the ideal of creation as the norm by which to understand the significance and role of the Mosaic permission to divorce. See Craig S. Keener, "Matthew," *The IVP New Testament Commentary* (Downers Grove, Ill.: InterVarsity Press, 1997), 294-99; Robert H. Gundry, *Matthew: A Commentary on His Literary and Theological Art* (Grand Rapids: Eerdmans, 1982), 375-88; Daniel J. Harrington, *Sacra Pagina: The Gospel of Matthew* (Collegeville, Minn.: The Liturgical Press, 1991), 272-76.

14. Charles H. Kraft, *Christianity in Culture: A Study in Dynamic Biblical Theologizing in Cross-Cultural Perspective* (Maryknoll, N.Y.: Orbis, 1981), 191-92, 398.

15. This is similar though not equivalent to Helmut Thielicke's distinction between creation orders that express the original intention and "emergency" orders put into effect as means of limiting the reign and effect of sin in creation (e.g., human politic, even human marriage becomes something to control human lust). These "emergency" orders are not on the same level as the creational orders but are certainly not sinful or demonic. They are less than God's intentional will but still acceptable to God within a fallen world where redemption is not yet completed in its full effects. See Helmut Thielicke, *Theological Ethics: Foundations, vol. 1* (Grand Rapids: Eerdmans, 1966), and *The Ethics of Sex* (London: John Clarke, 1963).

16. Walter Trobisch, *I Loved a Girl: Young Africans Speak* (New York: Harper and Row, 1963), develops the implications of Genesis 2:24 for marriage in detail. See also Walter Trobisch, *The Complete Works of Walter Trobisch* (Downers Grove, Ill.: InterVarsity Press, 1987).

17. Trobisch, *Complete Works*, 403.

18. Charles H. Talbert, *Reading Corinthians: A Literary and Theological Commentary on 1 and 2 Corinthians* (New York: Crossroad, 1987), 23-24.

19. Robin Scroggs, *The New Testament and Homosexuality* (Philadelphia: Fortress, 1983), offers an inadequate treatment of both Greco-Roman practices and ideals as well as New Testament reaction to them. Homosexuality cannot be reduced to pederasty nor can the objections of the New Testament be so narrowed as to refer only to pederasty. See also Michael Grant and Rachel Kitziner, *Civilization of the Ancient Mediterranean: Greece and Rome,* 3 vols. (New York: Scribners, 1988), esp. Jeffrey Henderson, "Greek Attitudes Toward Sex" (2:1249-63); Judith P. Hallett, "Roman Attitudes Toward Sex," 2:1265-78; Werner A. Krenkel, "Prostitution," 2:1291-97; Sarah B. Pomeroy, "Greek Marriage," 3:1333-42; Susan Treggiari, "Roman Marriage," 3:1343-54.

20. Henderson, "Greek Attitudes Toward Sex," 2:1254-55.

21. Ibid., 1258.

22. Talbert, *Reading Corinthians, 25.*

23. Note also Ovid's *Art of Love;* the epigrams of Catullus and Martial and poems about Priapus; Suetonius's biographies of the various emperors *(Lives of the Twelve Caesars,* "Nero" XXVII, 131-33, Loeb translation) with numerous extramarital affairs and homoerotic entanglements (Julius, 49; Augustus, 68; Nero 28-29) and even bestial forms of sexual entertainment.

24. Krenkel, "Prostitution," 2:1296.

25. The sort of professional prostitution found in the Greco-Roman world seems to have its origins in the sacred prostitution of Babylon and the ancient cult of Astarte. Leviticus 18 mentions idolatry in the same context as its strictures dealing with incest, homosexuality, and bestiality. But the rationale given for banning these practices is not explicitly because of their associations with idolatry. Rather, they are all commonly identified with practices of Egypt and Canaan and as violating the sovereign rights of Yahweh who redeemed and called Israel into holiness. The term *abomination* is linked first to idolatry in the midst of the covenant people and then to homosexuality. It is a religious term often used for cultic practices. Even in the New Testament there is a link between idolatry and homosexuality, but the rationale becomes much more explicit that it includes more than sacred, idolatrous ritual homosexuality and is linked to the Ten Commandments as a form of sexual immorality, not simply idolatry.

26. D. F. Wright, "Homosexuals or Prostitutes: The Meaning of *Arsenokoitai* [I Cor 6:9; I Tim 1:10]," *Vigiliae christianae* 38 [1984]: 105-24, shows the term for the active participant to refer to more than male sexual engagement with boys.

27. Talbert, *Reading Corinthians*, 25-26.

Chapter 2: Will Our Daughters Have Faith?

1. Conversation with Gary Haugen, author of *Good News about Injustice* (Downers Grove, Ill.: InterVarsity Press, 1999).

2. See Barbara Brown Zikmund, et al., *Clergy Women: An Uphill Calling* (Louisville: Westminster John Knox Press, 1998). For example, in the American Baptist Churches in the U.S.A. the number of women clergy rose from 157 in 1977 to 712 in 1994. The number of Presbyterian women clergy increased from 350 to 2,705 in the same period.

3. I am deeply indebted to Ron Sider and Evangelicals for Social Action for my growing understanding of the kingdom.

4. See Mary S. Van Leeuwen, *Gender and Grace: Love, Work, and Parenting in a Changing World* (Downers Grove, Ill.: InterVarsity Press, 1990).

5. These two movements are represented by Christians for Biblical Equality and the opposing Council on Biblical Manhood and Womenhood. See Ruth A. Tucker and Walter L. Liefeld, *Daughters of the Church* (Grand Rapids: Zondervan, 1987), on the history of the "daughters of the church."

6. Definitions of these terms are seldom agreed upon. I use them here to identify a spectrum that understands "fundamentalism" as the most conservative with the least openness to nontraditional roles for women in marriage, church, and society and "evangelical" as a diverse group of Christians, often within mainline pluralistic, as well as Holiness denominations, who are open to a wide variety of appropriate roles for women often including ordination and eldership in the local church.

7. For a very helpful resource on the challenges facing contemporary Christian women, see Rebecca Groothuis, *Women Caught in the Conflict: The Culture War between Traditionalism and Feminism* (Eugene, Ore.: Wipf & Stock Publishers, 1994).

8. See Gilbert Bilezikian, *Beyond Sex Roles: What the Bible Says about a Woman's Place in Church and Family*, 2d ed. (Grand Rapids: Baker, 1986), and other references on the biblical texts.

9. See Elizabeth Schüssler Fiorenza, *Bread, Not Stone: The Challenge of Feminist Biblical Interpretation* (Boston: Beacon Press, 1995).

10. The family is of course a more basic unit. See Van Leeuwen, *Gender and Grace*, 1990.

11. Christians for Biblical Equality can provide extensive bibliographies and helpful printed resources. They are located at 122 West Franklin Avenue, Suite 218, Minneapolis, MN 55404-2451.

Chapter 3: Inclusive Language and the Means of Grace

1. *Hamlet*, act 2, scene 2.

2. A. W. Tozer, *The Pursuit of God* (Wheaton, Ill.: Tyndale House, n.d.), 75.

3. See Herbert M. Carson, "The Covenant of Grace," in *Basic Christian Doctrines*, ed. Carl Henry (New York: Holt, Rinehart and Winston, 1962), 117-23.

4. Oswald Chambers, *Oswald Chambers: The Best from All His Books* (Nashville: Oliver-Nelson, 1987), 1:22.

5. Richard Foster, *Celebration of Discipline* (San Francisco: Harper and Row, 1988), 69.

6. Frank E. Gaebelein, "Other Means of Grace," in *Basic Christian Doctrines*, ed. Carl Henry (New York: Holt, Rinehart and Winston, 1962), 264.

7. So Donald Carson: "Because no two languages share exactly the same structure and vocabulary (and a lot of other things), it is impossible not to lose something when you translate an extended text from one language to another." *The Inclusive Language Debate* (Grand Rapids: Baker, 1998), 58.

8. Mark Strauss, *Distorting Scripture? The Challenge of Bible Translation and Gender Accuracy* (Downers Grove, Ill.: InterVarsity Press, 1998), 82. For example, unlike English, Hebrew and Greek nouns have grammatical gender. A word like *spirit* is feminine in the Hebrew and neuter in the Greek. But to translate spirit as "she" in the Old Testament and "it" in the New Testament would misrepresent meaning and be confusing to English-speaking readers. Words expressing biological gender (*male* or *female*) can be rendered literally, but words with grammatical gender will be rendered contextually in English.

9. John Kohlenberger, "Understanding the Current Controversy over Bible Translations," Paper presented at 1997 CBA International Convention, July 14, 1997 (privately printed, copyright John R. Kohlenberger III), 10.

10. Quoted in "Where All Is Babel, They Spread the Good Word," *New York Times,* May 20, 1997, A4.

11. Donald Carson, *The Inclusive Language Debate: A Plea for Realism* (Grand Rapids: Baker, 1998), 72.

12. "Questions and Answers about the New Translation, New International Version," New York International Bible Society: East Brunswick, N.J., n.d.

13. Quoted in *The Presbyterian Layman,* July/August 1984, 3.

14. Strauss, *Distorting Scripture?* 146.

15. Endorsement appearing on book cover of *The New Testament, Psalms, and Proverbs: Inclusive Language Edition, New International Version* (Hodder and Stoughton: London, 1995).

16. Kohlenberger, "Understanding the Current Controversy over Bible Translations," 23.

17. Strauss, *Distorting Scripture?* 94.

18. The Greek specifically uses *anthrōpos* (human being) for the form Christ took in the Incarnation, not *anēr* (a male being). The contrast Paul makes in Philippians 2:6-8 is not between the form of God and the form of a human male, or else the teaching would be that God's form is masculine, in direct contradiction of Scripture's declaration that God has no gender *(Deuteronomy 4:16)* and very specifically that God is not male *(Hosea 11:9).*

19. Roger R. Nicole, "The Savior and His Work," in *Applying the Scriptures,* ed. Kenneth Kantzer (Grand Rapids: Zondervan, 1987), 34-35.

20. Dietrich Bonhoeffer, *Life Together: A Discussion of Christian Fellowship* (San Francisco: HarperSanFrancisco, 1954), 24.

21. The Greek word used is the plural of *anthrōpos* (human being).

22. Henri J. M. Nouwen, *Reaching Out: The Three Movements of the Spiritual Life* (New York: Doubleday, 1986), 24, 65.

23. Carl Henry, *Carl Henry at His Best* (Portland, Ore.: Multnomah, 1989), 38.

24. Bonhoeffer, *Life Together,* 25-26.

25. Discussion of differing views concerning gendered language for God does not fall within the limits of this chapter. The conviction of this writer is that biblical language for God must be retained but that (as with words referring to humankind) we need to better understand the biblical meaning and intent, as well as to reclaim the entire scriptural range of language for God, such as metaphor, allegory, and symbolism.

Chapter 4: The Wounds of a Friend

1. "Perhaps the time is ripe for a new discipline that brings together sociology and theology. A scholar in one of our Christian colleges has given it a name—"sociotheology" (Tony Campolo, *Growing Up in America* [El Cajon, Calif.: Youth Specialties, 1994], 11).

2. Dr. Campolo has been a regular contributor to *Youthworker Journal,* as well as other magazines widely used by youth workers, such as *Group, Campus Life,* etc.

3. National Youth Workers Conventions are held twice yearly in separate locations. Sponsored by Youth Specialties (El Cajon, Calif.), they are the largest and most ecumenical of such annual gatherings of youth workers.

4. What is referred to in this chapter as "traditional" youth ministry is meant to refer to a status quo approach that is implicit in the vast majority of youth ministry literature and youth ministry practice. Because so much of youth ministry is resourced by the same handful of publishers and youth ministry thinkers, youth ministry practice tends to look quite similar across denominational lines. This would be true for parish-based and parachurch youth ministries.

Probably, most of what is written here could be said about youth ministry within the Roman Catholic tradition as well. (For a more thorough review of youth ministry within the Roman Catholic Church, see Charles Shelton, *Adolescent Spirituality* [Chicago: Loyola University Press, 1983].)

Having been personally involved in the youth ministry enterprise in South Africa, Australia, New Zealand, and in parts of Europe, I can say from experience that most of what is true about North American youth ministry is true about youth ministry in these non-North American countries as well. Some of this cross-pollination is good. Some of it, unfortunately, is not. While many of the strengths of North American youth ministry have been exported, so have some of its weaknesses. The observations set forth in this chapter, while they certainly have relevance for much of youth ministry outside of North America, are largely meant to refer to ministries within North America.

5. Half of all American teenagers attend a church worship service each week. As one might expect, the percentage of attendance decreases as the age of the adolescent increases. But, in fact, teenagers are more likely to attend a worship service than are adults. Two out of every three teenagers report that they pray at least once a week. One out of three teenagers reports that he or she reads the Bible during a typical week. In fact, unlike church attendance, the older the adolescent the more likely he or she is to read the Bible during the typical week. One out of every three teenagers participates in a Christian youth group in the course of a typical week. One out of every four teenagers takes part in a Bible study group of some sort, and almost four out of every ten teens show up at a Sunday school or catechism class each week (George Barna, *Generation Next* [Ventura, Calif.: Regal Books, 1995], 87-88).

6. Over three million teenagers nationally and internationally gathered around flagpoles on their campuses on September 15, 1999, for the annual "See You at the Pole" prayer event. On this tenth anniversary of the event a record number of teenagers gathered together before school to pray for their teachers, administrators, and peers.

7. "It should not be surprising that most teens admit that the chances of their leaving the Church are at least as good as the chances of staying. Only two of every five teens (41 percent) said they are 'very likely' to attend a church once they leave home. Roughly as many (36 percent) said they may attend, and the remaining one-quarter (22 percent) said the chances are slim to none....The teen segments who are most likely to predict their continued involvement with the church included 'A' students...girls, students living in the South, teens whose sociopolitical views are conservative and those currently connected with a Protestant church" (Barna, *Generation Next*, 92-93).

8. Ibid., 105.

9. As a youth worker, I have seen the value of Christian T-shirts, bracelets, bumper stickers, etc. My concern here is that too much of our teaching is reduced to what will fit on a T-shirt, bumper sticker, or bracelet. The bumper-sticker/T-shirt theology simply doesn't speak to the in-depth issues and questions that face today's adolescents.

10. David Seamands, *Putting Away Childish Things* (Wheaton, Ill.: Victor Books, 1983).

11. Kenda Creasy Dean and Ron Foster, *The Godbearing Life: The Art of Soul-Tending for Youth Ministry* (Nashville: Upper Room Books, 1998), 161.

12. Ibid.

13. Neil Postman, *Amusing Ourselves to Death* (New York: Viking Books, 1985), vii-viii.

14. For a provocative study of this idea, see Charles Sykes, *Dumbing Down Our Kids: Why American Children Feel Good about Themselves but Can't Read, Write or Add* (New York: St. Martin's Press, 1995).

15. Ibid., 3. Richard John Neuhaus cites a relevant comment made by the Catholic novelist Walker Percy back in 1990 as he responded to yet another attack on the narrow-mindedness and dogma of the Roman Catholic Church. Percy wrote, "These issues could be debated, as indeed they often are, but here's how it appears to one novelist. If such attacks continue and are successful, the result will be pleasing mainly to the secular liberal establishment, who are in fact calling the shots, and destructive and divisive to the Catholic people. This novelist can only observe that if the magisterium and the sacramental orthodoxy of the Church are compromised in the name of 'creative pluralism' or suchlike, there may be a lot of hugging and kissing and good feeling going on, but there won't be any Catholic novelists around. For these odd fellows are turned on precisely by these claims of the Church, breathtaking in their singularity and exclusivity, i.e., the magisterium and the Eucharist, and how these have endured with the people of God through these kinds of thicks and thins for two thousand years. And they will endure despite these chic brush-offs of 'Rome.' Get rid of 'Rome' and what will be left in the end is California" (*First Things*, October 1999, 99).

16. *The Business of Heaven*, ed. Walter Hooper (New York: Harcourt, Brace, 1984), 226.

17. This has not always been the case. In the mid-1980s through the early 1990s, for example, youth workers were able to choose from a variety of books that were intended to speak to the deeper issues of ministry, or at the very least, go beyond simply cataloguing ideas. For example, Youth Specialties alone published *Called to Care* (Douglas Stevens), *Feeding Your Forgotten Soul* (Paul Borthwick), *Intensive Care* (Rich Van Pelt), *High School Ministry* (Jim Burns and Mike Yaconelli), *Organizing Your Youth Ministry* (Paul Borthwick), *Youth Ministry Nuts and Bolts* (Duffy Robbins) and *Ministry of Nurture* (Duffy Robbins).

In recent years, however, one could leaf through the catalogue of Youth Specialties' published materials and find fewer than five books in the entire listing that actually used traditional prose as a format. All of the information was reduced to an idea and a paragraph about how to execute the idea. There were whole books on melodramas, small group ideas, and games, but very little that went deeper than could be expressed in a one-paragraph statement.

There are plans underway to develop a new "academic" line of books, and that is commendable. But what about products that will feed and stretch the rank-and-file youth worker beyond the academy? These are needed as well. It is difficult to think about big ideas in little paragraphs.

18. Eugene Peterson, *Working the Angles* (Grand Rapids: Eerdmans), 10-13.

19. Ibid., 10.

20. Ibid., 11.

21. I have personally benefited as a youth worker from many of Youth Specialties' excellent products along these lines. And as an author, I have been part of the development of many such products.

22. In 1996 Youth Specialties published a book entitled *Youth Ministry Crash Course.* The authors, Rick Bundschuh and E. G. Von Trutzschler, are widely respected, veteran youth workers, who have produced other published materials and spoken at training seminars in which their sense of professionalism and spiritual depth is quite evident. But in this particular work, with its encyclopedic style, listing a topic and giving a brief word of comment, the material is so diluted and dumbed down as to be virtually useless. For example, under the topic, "Spiritual growth" we read: "The kid that grows the fastest doesn't necessarily grow the deepest. Don't overlook the kid who grows slowly but steadily"—two lines attributed to this topic.

Earlier in the book, when the topic was "Points" (as in attributing points for scoring in games) the entry required just under half a page with additional cross-references to two other topics: "Choosing Teams" and "Games." Whether this was a decision of the publisher or the authors, I don't know. I do know that these two savvy youth workers with their wealth of experience could have given us so much more. But why do heart surgery if someone is only requesting an aspirin?

Chapter 5: Why Would Anybody Ever Want to Be an Evangelical?

1. For an excellent presentation of the logic of Christian claims, see C. Stephen Evans, *The Historical Christ and the Jesus of Faith* (Oxford: Clarendon Press, 1996).

2. Gary R. Habermas and Anthony G. N. Flew, *Did Jesus Rise from the Dead? The Resurrection Debate* (New York: Harper, 1987), 3.

3. Quoted in Joachim Jeremias, *New Testament Theology* (London: SCM, 1971), 175-76.

4. Reginald H. Fuller, *The Formation of the Resurrection Narratives* (New York: Macmillan, 1971), 2.

5. Pinchas Lapide, *The Resurrection of Jesus: A Jewish Perspective* (Minneapolis: Augsburg, 1983), 16.

6. Ibid., 125.

7. Robert Grant, *Historical Introduction to the New Testament* (New York: Harper, 1963), 376.

8. Wolfhart Pannenberg, *Jesus: God and Man* (Philadelphia: Westminster, 1968), 100 (Althaus's italics).

9. C. F. D. Moule, ed., "The Significance of the Message of the Resurrection for Faith in Jesus Christ," in *Studies in Biblical Theology,* no. 8 (London: SCM, 1968), 9.

10. E.g., Fuller, *Formation of the Resurrection Narratives, 10.*

11. Ernst Bloch, *Das Prinzip Hoffnung,* 2d ed. (Frankfurt am Main, Sukhrkamp Verlag, 1959), 2:1360ff., quoted in Pannenberg, *Jesus: God and Man,* 84.

12. See my *Just Generosity: A New Vision for Overcoming Poverty in America* (Grand Rapids: Baker, 1999).

Chapter 6: Higher Ground

1. The death penalty in the United States was temporarily ended in 1972 after the United States Supreme Court's decision in *Furman v. Georgia,* 408 U.S. 238 (1972), held that capital punishment was arbitrary, unpredictable, and too capricious to meet American constitutional requirements. While the court could have permanently ended the death penalty by declaring that it violates the U.S. constitutional prohibition against punishments that are "excessive" or "cruel and unusual," the court declined to take this approach.

2. These countries are Iran, Yemen, Pakistan, Saudi Arabia, Nigeria, and the United States.

3. There may have been as many as seventy-four juveniles on death row as of October 1998 (Victor L. Streib, *The Juvenile Death Penalty Today: Death Sentences and Executions for Juvenile Crimes, January 1973-October 1998* [Claude W. Pettit College of Law, Ohio Northern University, Ada, Ohio], 1999, 9). The United States has the most juveniles awaiting execution on death row of any country in the world.

4. Eighteen is the minimum age in California, Colorado, Connecticut, Illinois, Kansas, Maryland, Nebraska, New Jersey, New Mexico, New York, Ohio, Oregon, Tennessee, and Washington. Seventeen is the minimum age in Georgia, New Hampshire, North Carolina, and Texas. Sixteen is the minimum age in Alabama, Arizona, Arkansas, Delaware, Florida, Idaho, Indiana, Kentucky, Louisiana, Mississippi, Missouri, Montana, Nevada, Oklahoma, Pennsylvania, South Carolina, South Dakota, Utah, Virginia, and Wyoming.

5. Paranoid ideation is a condition under which an individual has suspicions of being harassed and persecuted, often leading the afflicted individual to assault perceived enemies.

6. The study was conducted by Dr. Dorothy Otnow Lewis, a psychiatrist at the New York University School of Medicine, and Dr. Jonathan H. Pincus, chairman of neurology at the Georgetown University Medical Center. Amnesty International, *United States of America: The Death Penalty and Juvenile Offenders 1* (Supp. 1994): 73.

7. Arkansas, Colorado, Georgia, Indiana, Kansas, Kentucky, Maryland, Nebraska, New Mexico, New York, Tennessee, Washington, and the federal government forbid the execution of the mentally retarded.

8. In *Ford v. Wainwright,* 477 U.S. 399 (1986), the United States Supreme Court held that the insane cannot be executed, but failed to define "insane." Later decisions have adopted this standard set out by Justice Powell in his concurrence.

9. Denis W. Keyes and William J. Edwards, "Mental Retardation and the Death Penalty," 21 *MPDLR* 5, 687 (Sept.-Oct. 1997). The United States Constitution mandates that states may execute only those persons whose culpability and moral blameworthiness are proportional to the punishment. "Culpability" refers to a defendant's capacity to distinguish between right and wrong. Today courts determine that defendants are "death eligible" if there is at least a minimal showing of moral awareness and a basic comprehension that the criminal act was wrong.

10. See, e.g., Stephen Bright, "Counsel for the Poor: The Death Sentence Not for the Worst Crime but for the Worst Lawyer," *Yale Law Journal* 7 (May 1994): 103.

11. Despite the elaborate review process surrounding capital cases in the United States, there have been eighty-five documented cases to date of innocent people who have been wrongly sentenced to death for crimes they did not commit. Some of these innocent men and women came within hours of an execution before being spared. For every seven people executed in the United States, an innocent death row prisoner has been identified. This shockingly high rate of error has caused a few states to consider a moratorium on capital punishment but has left most proponents of the death penalty undeterred. Recent advances in DNA testing have played a role in identifying some of the innocent on death rows across the United States. However, police and prosecutorial misconduct, mistaken identifications, inadequate defense lawyering, and other inherent problems in the politicized, wealth-dependent system of American justice account for most of these unjust death sentences.

Chapter 7: From Protest to Covenant

1. Tony Campolo, "Concern for the Church," *Sojourners*, March-April 1996.

2. "Hunger in a Strong Economy," Center on Hunger and Poverty, Tufts University, January 20, 2000.

3. "America's Homeless," The Urban Institute, February 1, 2000.

4. "A Status Report on Hunger and Homelessness in America's Cities 1999," U.S. Conference of Mayors, December 1999.

5. "Shifting Fortunes," United for a Fair Economy (Boston, 1999).

6. "The Great Divide," United for a Fair Economy (Boston, 1999).

7. *Business Week,* April 19, 1999.

8. "Shifting Fortunes," United for a Fair Economy (Boston, 1999).

9. "Human Development Report 1998," United Nations Development Program.

List of Contributors

John David Burton is currently a visiting scholar at Princeton Theological Seminary in Princeton, New Jersey. Tony dedicated his book *How to Rescue the Earth Without Worshiping Nature* to John, his first mentor in ministry.

David A. Fraser is professor of sociology and Christian studies and the dean of international leadership and development at Eastern College in Saint Davids, Pennsylvania; as well, he is a visiting professor at Nairobi Evangelical Graduate School of Theology. He coauthored with Tony *Sociology Through the Eyes of Faith.*

Roberta Hestenes, former president of Eastern College, is senior pastor of Solana Beach Presbyterian Church in Solana Beach, California.

Gretchen Gaebelein Hull is a founding board member of Christians for Biblical Equality and an independent scholar and writer.

Duffy Robbins is associate professor of youth ministry at Eastern College.

Ronald J. Sider is president of Evangelicals for Social Action and professor of theology and culture at Eastern Baptist Theological Seminary in Wynnewood, Pennsylvania.

Bryan A. Stevenson, a graduate of Eastern College and of Harvard Law School, is the executive director of Equal Justice Initiative of Alabama in Montgomery, Alabama, and an assistant professor of law at New York University School of Law.

Jim Wallis is editor-in-chief of *Sojourners* magazine and executive director of Call To Renewal.

Books by Tony Campolo

A Denomination Looks at Itself, 1971
The Success Fantasy, 1980
Ideas for Social Action, 1983
The Power Delusion, 1983
A Reasonable Faith, 1983
It's Friday, but Sunday's Comin', 1984
Radical Discipleship, 1984
You Can Make a Difference, 1984
Partly Right, 1985
Who Switched the Price Tags? 1986
Seven Deadly Sins, 1987
20 Hot Potatoes Christians Are Afraid to Touch, 1988
We Have Met the Enemy and They Are Partly Right, 1988
Growing Up in America : A Sociology of Youth Ministry, 1989
*Things We Wish We Had Said: Reflections of a Father
    and His Grown Son,*
        with Bart Campolo, 1989

The Kingdom of God Is a Party, 1990
Conviction Compassion, 1991
50 Ways You Can Feed a Hungry World,
    with Gordon Aeschliman, 1991
How to Be Pentecostal Without Speaking in Tongues, 1991
Short Term Mission Handbook,
    with Greg McClung and Floyd Livingston, 1991
Wake Up America! : Answering God's Radical Call While Living in the Real World, 1991
50 Ways You Can Help Save the Planet,
    with Gordon Aeschliman, 1992
50 Ways You Can Share Your Faith,
    with Gordon Aeschliman, 1992
Everything You've Heard Is Wrong, 1992
How to Rescue the Earth Without Worshiping Nature: A Christian's Call to Save Creation, 1992
Sociology through the Eyes of Faith,
    with David A. Fraser, 1992
Church and the American Teenager: What Works and What Doesn't Work in Youth Ministry, 1993
50 Ways You Can Be Prolife, 1993
50 Ways You Can Reach the World,
    with Gordon Aeschliman, 1993
Carpe Diem: Seize the Day, 1994
101 Ways Your Church Can Change the World: A Guide to Help Christians Express the Love of Christ to a Needy World, 1994
You Can Make a Difference, 1994
Can Mainline Denominations Make a Comeback? 1995
Is Jesus a Republican or a Democrat? And 14 Other Polarizing Issues, 1995
Following Jesus Without Embarrassing God, 1997
Revolution and Renewal: How Churches Are Saving Our Cities, 2000